A GARDENER'S YEAR

By Fennel Hudson:

A MEANINGFUL LIFE
A WATERSIDE YEAR
A WRITER'S YEAR
WILD CARP
FLY FISHING
TRADITIONAL ANGLING
THE QUIET FIELDS
FINE THINGS
A GARDENER'S YEAR
THE LIGHTER SIDE
FRIENDSHIP
NATURE ESCAPE
BOOK OF SECRETS
THE PURSUIT OF LIFE

Fennel's Journal

No. 9

A GARDENER'S YEAR

By

Fennel Hudson

2025

FENNEL'S PRIORY LIMITED

Published by Fennel's Priory Limited

www.fennelspriory.com

Limited edition magazine published in 2013
eBook published in 2013
This first edition hardback published in 2025

Copyright © Fennel Hudson 2013, 2025

Fennel Hudson has asserted his right under the
Copyright, Designs and Patents Act 1988
to be identified as the author of this work.

All rights reserved. No part of this publication may be
reproduced, stored in a retrieval system or transmitted,
in any form or by any means, electronic, mechanical,
photocopying, recording or otherwise, without
the prior permission of Fennel's Priory Limited.

"Stop – Unplug – Escape – Enjoy"
and The Priory Flower logo are registered trademarks.

A CIP catalogue record for this book
is available from the British Library.

ISBN 978-1-909947-34-4

Available to purchase in other formats at
www.fennelspriory.com

Designed and typeset in 12pt Adobe Garamond Premier Pro.

CONTENTS

Introduction 1
The Makings of a Gardener 5
Room to Grow 15
Dig It! 23
Chicken Poo 31
One Man's Weed 39
Pricking Out 49
The Cottage Garden 57
A Naked Assault 65
Urban Greenery 73
Dust and Desire 81
The Size of One's Carrot 89
Gardener for Hire 97
The Good Life 105
Garden of Dreams 113
Learning from the Master 121
The Last Cast 129

About the Author 131
The Fennel's Journal Series 135

STOP – UNPLUG – ESCAPE – ENJOY

This book, and the series to which it belongs, is about freedom. It's also about the adventures to be had when pursuing one's dreams, developing and communicating one's self, and striving for a slow-paced rural life.

Fennel's Journal is your opportunity to take time out from the stresses of modern living, to stop the wheels for a while, unplug from the daily grind, escape to a quiet and peaceful place, and enjoy the simple life. Because of this, it should ideally be read in a distraction-free and relaxing environment: your 'safe place' where you can savour quality time and, if possible, delight in the beauty of the countryside.

That's why this book is pocket-sized, has a special waxy cover, and is printed using waterproof ink. It's designed to be taken with you on your travels. Don't store it in pristine condition upon a bookshelf; allow it to reflect the adventures you've had. Use a leaf as a bookmark and annotate the pages with ideas of how you will honour your right to 'never do anything that offends your soul'.

The more mud-splattered, grass-stained, and ink-scribbled this book becomes, the more you've demonstrated your ability to pursue a contented country life. So go on: live your life, be authentic, and always remember to 'Stop – Unplug – Escape – Enjoy'.

"Just living is not enough… One must have sunshine, freedom, and a little flower."

Hans Christian Andersen

INTRODUCTION

This Journal is about dreams: about what was, what is, and what will be. For that is what gardening, to me, is all about. As Marina Schinz said, "Gardening is an exercise in optimism. Sometimes, it is the triumph of hope over experience." While experience grows with our plants, we need hope to bring our gardens – and dreams – to life.

The front cover of this Journal contains an image that perfectly captures my message of hope. It shows an early spring scene, with life (in the form of daffodils) returning from the earth. I'm there, holding a spade that's older than me. It is a legacy of gardeners past and a reminder of earth yet to be cultivated. But look closer, and see my problem. Do you see two worrying things, there in full view? I do. Blatantly and ashamedly. The first is the rusted surface of the spade, which hasn't been used in years. Second is the thinness of my forearm. They both ask a question: has Fennel, whose name comes from his association with plants, taken early retirement? Whatever happened to the well polished spade and bulging muscles of his gardening youth? Has his stem withered and dried, to be but a remnant of its former self? Is he in the winter of his years, awaiting a flattening gale? Or is he lying dormant, awaiting the New Spring?

Ten years have passed since I retired from gardening; when I swapped a 17-year career in horticulture for a centrally heated (but internally frozen) office job. Where the constant air temperature, 'ambient' lighting, and 24/7 work ethic led to a seasonless and artificial existence – more akin to intense greenhouse production than life on the land. Fennel, at the age of 28, had joined the race to become an over-ripe and easily squashed tomato. I should never have 'sold out' in an attempt to better myself. But alas, my wallet has become accustomed to a moth-free existence and beats me into submission each time I consider a return to manual work. And I have grown accustomed to creature comforts. I couldn't imagine life without my collectable fountain pens, old books, fine tweeds, and decanter of Islay single malt. Even my leather-topped writing desk supports these words, both physically and metaphorically. I am what I am: a writer dreaming of a life I once had, wishing it to be real, while clinging to the wires (and bearing the fruits) of my training. But the yearning is real. I must garden.

Ralph Waldo Emerson said, "Dare to live the life you have dreamed for yourself. Go forward and make your dreams come true...judge of your natural character by what you do in your dreams." While I may never again be a full-time gardener, I can at least dream of doing so while gardening domestically and writing about the pleasures I encounter. As Elizabeth Lawrence wrote, "Gardening, reading about gardening, and writing

INTRODUCTION

about gardening are all one; no one can garden alone." So I shall immerse myself in the activity of growing things and write a Journal dedicated to gardening and the importance of dreams. One that brings an outdoor life closer to home. For a home, after all, is the heart of a happy life. And a garden provides the beat that keeps it going.

Whether you are a keen or reluctant gardener, or not a gardener at all, I ask that you roll up your sleeves and imagine your vision of paradise. This, in whatever form it takes, is your garden. Keep hold of the image; know it's every detail and piece together the elements that need creating or nurturing, so that when you get the chance, you can prepare the ground, sow the seeds, and make it real. Ours is a gardener's life, whether we realise it or not. And so, metaphors in place, let's get real and create our garden.

I

THE MAKINGS OF A GARDENER

*"We may think we are tending our garden,
but of course, in many different ways,
it is the garden and the plants
that are nurturing us."*

Jenny Uglow

Thirty-five years have passed since I created my first garden. The plot, which measured three-feet square, had in its centre a slate-walled and turf-roofed cottage, complete with glass windows and a working chimney. It was surrounded by a picket fence made from lollipop sticks, which contained a lawn, a flower border, a compost heap and a vegetable garden. I trimmed the lawn with scissors, planted the border with daisies plucked from the surrounding wilderness, and grew radishes in the veg plot. Quite an achievement for a four-year-old. It was my great pride and passion. I tended to it for hours, days and weeks.

That was back in 1978, a 'year of miracles', when U.S. Army Sergeant Walter Robinson walked across the English Channel (using homemade water shoes), Louise Brown became the world's first 'test tube' baby, and May Day became a bank holiday. But alas, bread rationing was put in place (following the bakers' strike), and the final series of The Good Life aired on television. The theme tune to this classic British sitcom had me running indoors whenever I heard it. In fact, it was one of the few things that would encourage me indoors (the others being teatime and the arrival of the morning – and afternoon – post). And there, in front of the television, I would be glued to every vision of self-sufficiency I could glimpse. I didn't realise it was a comedy, or that Felicity Kendal was the hottest thing ever to wear dungarees. I just imagined myself working that suburban garden, producing vegetables in the middle of winter (as they did), converting the cellar into a clanking, burping, methane burning heating system, and sipping eyesight-threatening Peapod Burgundy. It was my dream, and that of many in the 1970s. (Who were reacting to power cuts, a second recession, limited choice, lack of basic home comforts, and much political unrest.) But I was just four-years-old. I thought that regular huddles around a candle were all part of normal night-time routine. I craved not for central heating, a telephone, or a regular wage. I just wanted to garden. And in doing so, I began a lifelong love of all things horticultural.

Encouraged by my parents, I began to practise and study gardening. I was first taught to recognise the common garden weeds, and allowed to pull them from the borders. Then I was allowed to read my parents' copy of the 1946 picture book Adam the Gardener, which taught me the basics of what should be done in the garden each month. (It also showed me how to contain my excitement by pretending to be utterly miserable; such is its unromanticised view of the practicalities of post-war gardening.) With this as my guide, I was shown how to propagate and nurture many types of trees, shrubs, perennials, annuals and bulbs. My green fingers grew, along with calluses and a desire to tackle ever-larger gardening projects.

At the age of eleven, I started a Saturday job working as a gardener at a local country house. Here I was allowed to garden unsupervised. I was given free access to the potting shed, greenhouse and tool shed. Soon I was handling all sorts of things that would make a protective parent flinch with fear. Garden shears, scythes, secateurs, pruning knives, and petrol mowers were handled carefully but freely. 'Fish, Blood and Bone' was scattered by un-gloved hand and sandwiches were eaten straight after. But I survived, proud of my expertise and newfound freedom; confident in the knowledge that if, as the saying goes, we eat a peck of dirt before we die, then I'd eaten these two dry gallons of soil before I was out of short trousers.

I built a reputation, and small business, off the back of my weekend job, increasing the number of clients' gardens I tended to each week. By the age of 15 I was looking after seven gardens in my village, working all weekend plus three nights in the week; by 17 I had combined my artistic and gardening talents and was designing gardens up to five acres in size. At 18 I took the plunge and began a degree in landscape architecture. But it wasn't for me. All those planting

A GARDENER'S YEAR

designs for motorways and supermarket car parks, they were too industrial; too impersonal. So I switched to studying horticulture at Pershore College. This was the making of me. Here I learned about the importance of the soil and compost; about crop production and garden design; about plant physiology and pests; about garden history; and the origins and Latin naming of plants. And, most memorably, about identifying and understanding the natural flora of the British Isles – what grows where, and why – to be able to piece everything together based upon what grows naturally in an area. This, and my fascination with traditional garden design (I was strongly influenced by the books of Rosemary Verey and Penelope Hobhouse), led me to specialise in designing and maintaining gardens around historic or traditionally styled houses.

My first post-college appointment was as gardener at the prestigious Rooksnest Estate in Berkshire. The property, once the childhood home of The Avengers star Patrick Macnee, was the weekend retreat of Dr Mortimer Sackler – the tenth richest man in the world – and his wife, Dame Theresa Sackler. Here they entertained royalty; hosted garden parties, and accommodated a graduate gardener who couldn't believe his luck. The internationally famous garden designer Arabella Lennox-Boyd had designed the ten acres of formal gardens, herb garden, vegetable garden, woodland garden and glasshouses. They were maintained by five full-time gardeners, of which I had primary responsibility for a one-acre rose garden. Here I was able to learn from Arabella's masterly planting designs and their relationship with the building and its owners. It accelerated my career in garden design, which I ran in parallel to my time at the estate. I designed 'Arabella-style' gardens for clients in five countries (one of these was a 30-acre garden adjacent to the National Palace in the Sintra Hills of Portugal). I then received an offer of work from respected garden designer David Stevens. I turned him down (rather foolishly) and instead became a full-time, self-employed, designer.

I designed a Capability Brown style landscape with lake, parkland and a four-acre walled garden for the producer of BBC's Countryfile. And then, just as the media was noticing me, I bowed out of the limelight. Life had become a pretentious whirlwind of name-dropping and ever-growing snobbishness. I was designing increasingly large and 'showy' gardens that were meant to be looked at, rather than lived in. My initial bond with the earth and plants was lost, replaced by a light bulb poised over a drawing board and constant dealing with customers who wanted 'instant' gratification. A minority of homeowners had gardens suitable for my style of design, but became less as fashions changed with the popularity of 'garden makeover' TV shows. They changed people's expectations of what could be achieved on a budget. Customers started asking me to incorporate decking, artificial grass and blue fencing into my designs. Then they began asking me how much their garden would cost to build. Times were changing. I retracted from the garden design scene, packing away my drawing board and looking instead for something that brought me back into contact with gardeners who

actually gardened, who wanted to dirty their hands in honest soil, and see the fruits of their labours rather than someone else's.

My old college contacted me, saying there was a job going as a researcher for a gardening television programme. They needed someone to trawl their library of plant images for use in the weekly show. I didn't see how the job could lead anywhere (I can be a complete idiot at times), and so, I am told, my fellow Pershore student Chris Beardshaw took the role. He ended up presenting the programme and winning gold medals at The Chelsea Flower Show; while I went to work as deputy manager of a garden centre, where I stocked shelves and collected squeaky-wheeled trolleys from the car park. While I loved the daily contact with gardeners, I found – to my surprise – that the majority of sales at the garden centre did not come from plants (which represented only 30% of turnover). They came from seasonal products (such as barbeques and Christmas items), furniture and giftware. As I sold my umpteenth conservatory sofa, I realised I might as well have been working in a department store. I quit my job at the garden centre, and went to work for a plant nursery.

Bransford Garden Plants (now Bransford-Webbs) specialises in growing and supplying potted plants to garden centres. I worked there for four happy years, having responsibility for their marketing activities. I wrote and sourced images for plant labels, posters and brochures, which promoted the new plant releases each year. I wrote articles and press releases for magazines, hosted media days and exhibitions, managed sales campaigns and toured garden centres to promote our 'seasonal best'. It was a lovely life. And I did well. Horticulture Week (the industry's trade magazine) hailed me as 'the UK's top horticultural marketer'. And yet I earned little more than the minimum wage. This wasn't a problem until 2001, when I was refused a mortgage on the grounds of my 'poor earnings'. This opened my eyes to the necessities of life, and the need to earn a decent wage. I quit my job at the nursery and went freelance, throwing myself into a fast-paced career in marketing. I was successful. Eager. And idiotic. Within two years of leaving the nursery, my life had spiralled out of control. By giving my all to my career, I had lost everything else. I became homeless, jobless, and in poor health. (If you've read my book 'A Meaningful Life', you'll know how and why this happened, and what came next.) Feeling wounded, and in dire need of money, I went to work in a city. There, amongst the pollution and noise, I forgot about the warm perfumed breeze of a garden.

It was Mahatma Gandhi who said, "To forget how to dig the earth and to tend the soil is to forget ourselves." True to his warning, I became a shadow of my former self. My skin paled, my waistline grew, and my hair thinned. I felt empty. But I found peace outside of work – in quiet fields and fine things. However, after ten years living a part-time life, I now feel the need to garden. Not 'once more', but 'forever more'. It is time to prune back a decade's worth of spindly light-starved growth, and leave only a single growing tip through which I can focus my energy.

As I approach my 40th birthday, and question what life is all about, I can't help but angle my ear towards open windows in the hope that I'll hear the upbeat theme tune of my favourite TV programme. The Good Life has always been there, in the background, but now it's getting louder once again. Do you hear it? Me too.

JANUARY

II

ROOM TO GROW

"Show me your garden and I shall tell you what you are."
Alfred Austin

A garden is where we, and our plants, can grow. But at this time of year, there isn't much happening in the garden. Sure, there's plenty of colour from the cyclamen and aconites, and the naked stems of willow and dogwood glow radiantly in the evening sunlight, but our gardens are mostly dormant. Mine is more dormant than most. In fact, it's sulking.

The garden where I presently reside is small and suffers from having a disadvantaged start in life. It is one of those 'pocket handkerchief' plots reluctantly provided by modern housing developers who, when they created this garden, simply laid twelve inches of weed-infested subsoil over the tarmac of an old car park, threw in their leftover rubble, and then covered it with half-dead turf. It's north facing, too, so doesn't get much direct sunlight; and it's waterlogged due to the tarmac beneath. But it's mine. So I try to love it, and spend time in it. Sadly, so does next door's cat. So I'm constantly reminded of the slow decay (and smell) of cat poo that lies half-buried in sodden soil. My garden deserves better.

At seventeen feet long by fourteen feet wide, my garden is smaller than my living room. It's barely large enough to house a shed, support a table and four chairs, grow a few plants, and please its owners. But it does. Just. As they say, 'I've had better, but will make the most of what I've got'.

Mrs H and I moved here five years ago as part of our search for a better life. We'd got new jobs and dreamed of living in The Cotswolds. Our new home was on the edge of the area we loved, and was a logical choice for people with little time and even less money. There were compromises, for sure, but overall we were pleased with what we got. We set to work on the garden, erecting trellising and a pergola, laying paving, and building a shed. We removed six wheelbarrow-loads of rubble and two of couch grass roots, replacing them with rich and wonderful soil-conditioning compost. Several shade-loving plants were planted, so we could enjoy seeing foliage in the garden. Ferns, hostas, hydrangeas, jasmines and hellebores grew well. We even planted several shrub roses, though I knew they weren't happy. (They looked like elegant ladies forced to do their shopping at Crusty Bob's Bargain Basement.) I experimented with containers and hanging baskets, managing to grow fuchsias, pelargoniums, lobelia and petunias; also radishes, beetroot, runner beans, French beans, mange tout, early and main crop potatoes, carrots and – during one especially warm summer – a glut of cherry tomatoes. I've also grown parsley, mint, sage, thyme and strawberries. Oh, and a somewhat leggy and anaemic-looking rosemary. But pride and joy, and with overwhelming success, has been the two autumn fruiting raspberry bushes planted in four inches of soil next to the house. This is the one and only spot that gets a glimmer of direct sunlight (for about twenty minutes each evening). I mulched this area with compost and topped it up each day with the 'deposit' from the cat. The result has been a treat of twenty raspberries daily from October through to December. Little Lady Hudson has loved them, and – as is the way in town gardens – we have zero threat from birds (which feed elsewhere, where green corridors bring life into the town). We are proud of these raspberries. They have given us a taste, quite literally, of how satisfying homegrown produce can be.

But let's get real. My garden is small. Too small for a lawn, or a sizeable pond, or a vegetable plot large enough to rotovate. Too tiny for a proper compost heap or bonfire area, and too weeny to grow a prize-winning pumpkin. So what chance do we have to turn our back on the supermarket and grow our own food?

In his 1975 book entitled A Cottager's Companion, D. S. Savage made it clear that "In any cottage way of life the garden is the most important thing…The larger the garden the greater the degree of self-support which will be possible. A cottage which has in addition to a garden, a meadow or orchard, or grazing rights on common land, offers much greater opportunities. An intending cottager should always try for as large a parcel of land as possible when negotiating for a dwelling."

A meadow or orchard? Grazing rights? My garden

is not so much 'large parcel' as 'crumpled envelope'. Mrs H and I have little chance of becoming self-sufficient, or horticulturally satisfied. Our gardening life is what it is: a rather stumpy parsnip with an appendage that looks – to all observers – like a withered and contorted willy.

Geoff Hamilton, the respected TV gardener and writer, wrote, "There is nothing like a garden for making you feel small. There you are, right in the middle of the greatest miracle of all – the world of growing things." And so I feel encouraged by what I've got. It might not be the sort of thing to mention to new friends (delivered, legs astride, eyebrows raised, with a suave "what do you think of that, baby?") but I might as well tell you about it anyway. We are, after all, friends with a shared interest. I suppose what I'm saying is that my current garden is the

best it can be, and that my future garden will be better. Not that I feel short-changed. As the garden designer Gertrude Jekyll said, "The size of a garden has very little to do with its merit. It is the size of the owner's heart and brain and goodwill that will make his garden either delightful or dull." So I'm focused on what will be, in my garden of the future.

Francis Hodgson Burnett said, "To write as one should of a garden one must write not outside it or merely somewhere near it, but in the garden." And so, in the spirit of tradition, I am writing these words from my garden. To be precise, I am writing them from the relative warmth of my garden shed. I call this space 'the potting shed' although, in reality, it is home to all manner of clutter and is used principally as a bolthole for when I need a bit of quiet time. Such is the real purpose of a shed. It is man domain, where we men may delude ourselves that we are masters of our homes and can do whatever we want, whenever we want. For in our shed, we can relax, knowing that The Lady of the House doesn't understand or question our activities. We may tinker with engines; sharpen, clean or restore tools; sow seeds and transplant seedlings; smoke a crafty pipe or cigar; sip from a secretly-stashed hip flask; study the form of horses running in the 2.30 at Ascot; or, if we're lucky, partake in whatever obligations we may have with Lady Chatterley. What a man does in his shed is his business. Nobody else's. So I'm making an exception by writing to you from this sacred place.

I told Mrs H that I was nipping to the shed to oil a tool or two. (I did, after all, use my secateurs and loppers on twelve occasions last year.) She gave me the look of someone hearing a feather drop in a library. Unconcerned by my absence, she continued reading her book. So I snuck out here, into the cat-pong-shady-place, where I have felt the bracing cold of winter and the warmth of a large brandy. I'm writing these words to you while my hands remain warm and my 'spirit' is high.

If there's a key learning in life, it is this: "When you get down, you get back up; fast!" Such are my thoughts on this dim and frosty January day. It's a quiet time of year, which provides opportunity for us to plan for the year ahead. We may decide which plants and seeds we will purchase; how the ornamental and production areas of our garden will look and be used, and any changes to the garden's structure that may be required.

Indeed, anything that sets seed in our mind while we sit and think about what will come, and how we can enhance our enjoyment of our garden. My thoughts are focused on what garden Mrs H and I will have when we return to cottage life. For this is our plan, to be realised within the next eighteen months. While our town house has served as a valuable commuter base, it is not suitable for family life or the needs of a countryside writer. So we shall move, to somewhere with more character. And a bigger, sunnier, and pleasant-smelling garden.

My dream is for a little cottage adjacent to fields and woods, where I may live in harmony for the rest of my years. I'll grow lavenders and pinks alongside the paths; wisteria and rambling roses will adorn the walls; the borders will be filled with hollyhocks, delphiniums, poppies, geraniums and peonies. And my vegetable and fruit garden will help to put fresh food on our plates each day. I'll have a writing den and a potting shed; there will be a greenhouse, chicken hut, compost bins, water butts and – if I'm lucky – an outdoor lavvy. I might even build a larder of sorts, where I can hang game, store fruit and vegetables, house shelf upon shelf of jams, chutneys, hams, salami, and pickles; and brew some rocket-powering real ale. Ultimately, and because of the planning I'm doing now, this future garden will be home to my dreams. In fact, it will fulfil a promise I made many years ago, to lead an uncompromised and fulfilling life.

So, as I sit here in my potting shed, I realise that wherever we may be, we will always have room to grow.

February

III

DIG IT!

*"A real gardener is not a man who cultivates flowers;
he is a man who cultivates the soil."*

Karel Capek

I am writing this with my trousers around my ankles and my pants around my knees, while I sit bare-bottomed on the soil of my diminutive vegetable garden. I am trying to ascertain whether the numbness in my buttocks is caused by me sitting here for too long, or because the ground is much cooler than I expected for this mild February day. Either way, it seems that my bum has gone on strike and I am in danger of risking a serious attack of pins and needles.

I am doing this for a reason, trying to determine whether the ground is warm enough to sow seeds, or if it needs longer to warm up. Tradition dictates that if the ground is too cold to sit upon comfortably, then it's too early to sow; but if it feels warm and comfortable, then the time is right to scatter one's vegetable seed. It sounded straightforward in the book: putting it into practice would simply require a quick squat while Mrs Stroppup, my nosy and garden-hating middle-aged neighbour, isn't watching me through her upstairs window; a slight wiggle in the dirt, and I ought to know instantly whether I felt comfortable or not. But, sadly for me (and to Mrs Stroppup's horror), I am not a quick decision maker. The ground felt damp, for sure. And a bit claggy as it worked its way between my cheeks. But it didn't feel especially cold. Or warm. Just strange. So I decided to sit for a while longer, waiting for my bum and brain to speak to one another. And then I got comfortable. I gave Mrs Stroppup a wave, as she stared at me through her upstairs window, then casually parted my legs, placed my notebook in my lap, and began writing this month's journal.

You might think my behaviour to be eccentric. But my actions are based upon logic. There is much sense in checking the warmth of the soil before sowing seeds. No point scattering early for them to just rot in the soil. But logic would say that February is way too early to sow. We're still having regular frosts, and there's every chance of snowfall. But I'm eager to get going in the garden. Or, to be more precise, to get growing. I want to be doing something productive.

While a low maintenance garden is okay for most working people, I crave a high maintenance garden, one that will constantly challenge me, encouraging me outdoors, away from a computer screen and the comfort of an office chair. One that will give me something purposeful and physical to do when I need a break from writing. (It sounds like a lot of work, but it's not. At least not to the impassioned gardener. As Dorothy Gilman wrote, "What astounds me about a garden is that you can walk past it in a hurry, see something wrong, stop to set it right, and emerge an hour or two later breathless, contented, and wondering what on earth happened.")

The result of my actions? My bum is shouting loudly to my brain that it is frozen to the point of numbness, but my mind doesn't want to listen. And so I will sit here until I'm absolutely convinced (and numbed to the coccyx) that it is worth sowing just one or two seeds, or planting some bulbs, or 'borrowing' Mrs H's hairdryer and warming the soil a little. Stubbornness will prevail, even if it means me having bum cheeks that look and feel like frozen marshmallows. First though, I will finish this chapter; then I will bear the agony of cramp and hobble indoors to ask Mrs H if she wouldn't mind helping me 'adjust' to the comfort and cleanliness of our home by dabbing my bottom with a warm soapy sponge.

Don't get me wrong. I don't mind getting dirty in the garden. In fact I love it. As Margaret Attwood wrote, "In the spring, at the end of the day, you should smell like dirt." Little Lady follows her daddy's love of gardening, liking digging as much as I do. She describes it, with a scrunched up nose and hands held aloft, as getting "good dirty!" And that's from a two-year-old who definitely knows best. Good honest soil is honest. And it keeps us so, too.

Every experienced gardener knows that the soil in their garden is their most valuable resource. Without it, their green-fingered activities would be futile, like going swimming in a pool with no water, or hang-gliding in a sky with no air. Our soil is precious, and requires looking after. It's also worth understanding the soil, so that you know how to care for it.

I could mention here about the value of soil testing kits, of needing acid soil for ericaceous plants (such as heathers, skimmias, and rhododendrons) or chalky soil for lime loving plants (such as ceanothus or delphiniums), or the scientific way of measuring the organic content of soil. But I'm not. Instead, I recommend that you just do what's obvious: put an acorn-sized ball of wet soil in the palm of your hand, then press and roll it with the thumb of your other hand. If the ball crumbles then it's probably sandy or gritty (and most likely acidic, unless you can see chalky limestone in it); if it smears or becomes putty-like then it has a clay content (which commonly is limey). And there's every chance you'll have something in between, such as a sandy loam or clay loam. Next, check the organic matter in the soil. Is it dark and earthy-smelling? Can you see any bits of leaves or woody material? Would it burn if placed in a metal spoon that's held over a flame? Organic matter, known as humus, is good. This is what helps to release the nutrients from the soil, opens up its texture to allow plant roots to explore, and helps retain and drain water in the soil. It's important, so if you haven't got much organic matter in your soil, get some in, quick; either in the form of compost or well-rotted manure.

The soil in my garden is known to most as clay loam. But I call it Arthur. Arthur seemed a good name for soil that was only half as good as I'd have liked. When I first dug into it, it smelled stagnant and felt sticky. I called it Arthur Gawnorf. It was humus free subsoil, no good for plants. (Only the top eight inches of soil are nutrient and humus rich, due to the excellent work done by our earthworm friends*. The soil below serves mostly to anchor the plant and retain water. The builders, who laid this ground, had used subsoil from deep excavations.)

*"*The earth without worms,*" wrote naturalist Gilbert White, "*would soon become cold, hard-bound, and void of fermentation, and consequently sterile.*" He was right. Worms are the gardener's true friend, along with bees for pollination, ladybirds for aphid control, and hedgehogs for after-dark slug munching.*

Arthur and I developed a love-hate relationship from the off. He lay there, all lumpy and full of bricks, cockily challenging me to 'do my best'. I responded by attacking him with a spade and burying him beneath eight barrow-loads of shop-bought compost. A day of double digging, single forking and triple swearing (when I discovered the tarmac underneath) saw Arthur transformed into a half-decent plot of loose and fluffy earth. Just right for next-door's moggy to sink its bum into and, come to that, for me too. (I still can't decide whether this soil feels like a bag of frozen peas, or chilled Plasticine, or a stale loaf. In fact, the last time my bum felt like this, I was two-years-old, sitting in the snow in a rather stiff and stinky nappy, wondering what the hell just happened to my sledge.)

I digress. Back to the scene at hand.

Mrs Stroppup is now tapping her window and pointing at my ankles, as if they were doing something I wasn't aware of. She has the look of a woman who detests the outdoors, simply because there's too much grime for her vacuum cleaner to cope with.

I can play her game. I could stand up quickly, lift my notebook and gyrate my hips, swinging my 'dibber' from side to side while holding my hand in the air and rotating it towards her, doing my best 'dance floor lasso' move? No. She's too old, and I'm too cold, for that. And besides, I'd probably get into trouble with the neighbourhood watch. And Mrs H.

What to do then? Right. I have an idea. Let me try it, and I'll report back.

Deed done.

I looked up towards Mrs Stroppup, put my hand to my ear and shook my head, implying that I couldn't hear what she was saying. She opened the window, and with an indignant snort, shouted, "Pervert!" I raised my hands, but before I could reply, she hit me with, "I suppose you're going to sit there all day, aren't you? Chilling your bits until they're ready to drop off? And drop off they will, mark my words. Just look at what happened to my Malcolm when we went on our second honeymoon. It was supposed to be a romantic skiing holiday. Not so for him. Not after that night on the peach schnapps and the incident with the ski pole. There was no ski lift or rides of any description after that. So pull your trousers up and stop trying to prove something. You men are all the same. Soft in the head and even softer everywhere else!" At that, she grabbed the window and began to pull it shut. Then she paused, and shouted, "By the way; that smell? Is it you, or the cat?"

Hmm. It seems that being a traditional gardener has its limitations, especially for one's reputation with the neighbours. Best I keep my activities secret, or confined to the privacy of my shed. So I am compelled to stand up (discretely) and stare back at the buttock furrow I've created in the soil.

Aah. There it is: the expected furrow, dimpling (or dumpling?) me into shame. It seems that Arthur Gawnorf has won this latest round in the battle for soil supremacy, reminding me that I'm not in the best of shape, and that the soil is too wet to sow. I will cower from view and retreat indoors, grubby-cheeked and ashamed.

But what will I tell Mrs H? I can't admit to a pointless exercise that has caused me so much grief. I must have a reason.

"Ah," and excuse the pun, "soddit". I'm going to sow those seeds anyway, even if I have to wait six weeks to see any growth.

As William Robinson said, I "have no patience with bare ground… let little ground plants form broad patches and colonies…" I shall show Arthur who's boss, even if it takes a little 'barefaced cheek' to do it.

March

IV

CHICKEN POO

Gertrude Jekyll wrote, "The main purpose of a garden is to give its owner the best and highest kind of earthly pleasure." Well, after last month's extended winter sit-in on my vegetable plot, I can confirm that I did not receive the best kind of 'earthly' pleasure. Not at all. I acquired chilblains in places where one can only show the doctor, a weeklong inability to sit on hard surfaces, and a fortnight's worth of jibbing from my neighbour. From now on, when it comes to testing the temperature of my soil, I shall do it with my hand or a thermometer. And I'll wait until my neighbours have gone out. But now, after a month, I can sit without crying and walk without wincing. I can also look my garden, and neighbours, in the face. Everything's back as it should be. Which is a good thing. Because, right now, I'm faced with the need to talk through my backside and look people firmly in the eyes.

I'm in the middle of an executive dinner party at a posh 'Michelin Star' restaurant (read 'tiny portions of offal, sold to people who want to spend more time talking about the food than actually eating it), held in honour of me and my colleagues who have, it appears, become toast of the company for our hard work and successes. The party is halfway through an entrée of bravado and ego sparring, and about to consume a main course of one-upmanship and belittlement. Which is why I've chickened out of the conversation, and snuck off to the aromatic confines of the restaurant toilet. Here I have found a place to sit and rest, and write these words. But unlike last month, I do not have my trousers around my ankles. Instead, I am sitting on the firm seat of the toilet, fully clothed and doing my best to spend as much time in here as possible. You see, I find business events like this to be taxing. It's not that I dislike my colleagues, or shy away from public gathers – far from it – it's just that attendees at such events seem obliged to make the most ridiculous conversation.

Tonight's event is attended by twelve people. There are ten salesmen, a business manager (me) and a commercial manager. We sat down to eat, and then did the usual 'round the table' introductions. Job titles were mentioned which, given the international nature of our business, included all manner of Regional, Multinational, Global and Presidential titles. (If our managers had been there, we'd have included titles such as Intergalactic Emperor, and Supreme Ruler of the Universe; such is the pretentiousness of business cards that have to be twice folded before they can fit into one's wallet.) That done, conversation moved to, "So what you drivin' at the moment?" My answer of "Nothing at the moment; I'm just sitting here awaiting my dinner," was not well received, especially when I heard what other people were driving. The list was so staggering – and alien to me – that I wrote it down on a napkin.

CHICKEN POO

My notes were as follows: Porche 911 Carrera, Mercedes-Benz SL 65, Jaguar XFR-S, Aston Martin DB9 Volante, Audi R8 V10, Lexus LFA, Maserati Granturismo, BMW M6 Gran Coupe, Lamborghini Gallardo LP, Ferrari Berlinetta; and my favourite answer, "Nissan Micra – naught to sixty in twenty-eight seconds – I'm in the wife's car!" said by the commercial manager, who was keen to save pennies.

Then, as the pecking order was becoming clearer, the salesmen asked each other "How many bedrooms does your house have?" The best answer, said by the salesman whose gold watch was pinning his arm to the floor, was "Thirty-three. I've got six houses around the world so that I don't have to stay in hotels when I'm travelling." (To which our response was, "Who cleans all those bedrooms? Your wife?" He replied with, "Er, no. She left me. I've got cleaners." To which we said, "Sounds painful. Have you seen a doctor?")

CHICKEN POO

The party eventually ordered their food, began drinking their champagne, and started to relax. And it was here that the conversation got weird.

It seems that given the chance we each have an inner nerd, waiting to get out. All that's required is someone to ask us about our hobbies. The salesmen with the cars were, most predictably, petrol heads with a thirst for speed. To my left, the conversation was focusing on the weight-to-speed benefit of removing the seats from one's car and replacing them with titanium-framed plastic buckets. To my right, where the commercial manager was sitting, there was talk was of the business risk of using a solar-powered calculator in low light conditions. One guy had visited all the 'geo-cache' locations between Bristol and London, noting the size, colour and quality of any caches made from Tupperware boxes. And, typical for telecoms employees, there was round-the-room discussion about how tethering an Android can be more satisfying than inserting a broad-banded dongle.

And then, after avoiding eye contact for a good while, they asked me the inevitable question: "So, Fennel, tell us what really does it for you."

"Really?" I replied, leaning back in my chair. "What really does it? In a really gets me going sort of way?"

"Yes."

"What really gets me going?"

"Yes."

"Okay. As you've asked, and with advance warning. The thing I'm really into, is poo."

"Eh? What the? You shittin' us?"

"I suppose so. But in a literal way."

"Bull!"

"No, chicken, actually."

The room went quiet. Someone dropped a spoon. And a lady at the table next to us asked a waiter if she and her husband could move elsewhere.

It was Hugh Popham who said, "Gardeners, like infants, are proud of their waste products." So, as eleven open mouths gasped at me from around the table, I could think of only one thing to say: a quote by William Longgood. "I personally like manure." I said, calmly. "I never feel so affluent as when bringing back the occasional load of high-class dung." To which I added, "Especially if it is chicken poo, dried or composted so that it smells sweet and crumbles between one's fingers. That fresh stuff is no good; it can stain your hands and its alkalinity can scorch your plants. But the dry stuff, wow. It's amazing: 4% nitrogen, 2% phosphorous, and 1% potassium – depending, of course, on the diet and health of your chickens and the water content of the manure – it's what's needed to produce both leafy and root growth, and encourage flowering. And poultry manure releases up to 75% of its nitrogen content in the first year, compared to only 33% from most other manures. Which is great, as every gardener knows that you feed the soil, not the plant. So you can keep your 'fast food' chemical fertilisers that encourage lush growth that's easily attacked by pests and diseases; they're not for me. A good handful of chicken manure. That's what really does it for me."

The mouths closed, smiles formed, and laughter was

heard. I got the vote for being the biggest nerd in the room.

When dessert arrived, and we saw that it was a gloopy-looking 'chocolate log', I was forced to confess that dung from protein-eating animals is not recommended for use on the compost heap (due to the risk of parasites entering the food chain). As a regular eater of meat, I could not produce my own compost, at least for use on the vegetable or herb garden. (Even though I risk it by putting cat poo on my raspberries.) Which gave me the opportunity to excuse myself. I got up and retreated to the chipboard sanctuary of a cubicle in the restaurant toilet. And I've been here ever since, in a place of 'wasted waste', with its sterile tiles and low lighting (marked '35 watts, do not remove'). I feel a million miles from the welcoming, organic, and sunny paradise of a garden.

You might think me vulgar, and a little nerdy, for writing about this subject – and in such an unromantic place, too. But as D. H. Lawrence wrote, "The fairest thing in nature, a flower, still has its roots in earth and manure." So here I shall sit, until my party notices I'm missing or chicken manure becomes as trendy as a designer sports car. Or, given where I'm sitting, I could shout "Poo!" and start an organic 'movement'?

April

V

ONE MAN'S WEED

"I am not a lover of lawns. Rather I would see daisies in their thousands, ground ivy, hawkweed, and even hated plantain with tall stems, and dandelions with splendid flowers and fairy down, than the too-well-tended lawn,"

W. H. Hudson

It's interesting to consider what motivates us in the garden. I am, as you have discovered, a fan of compost and organic fertiliser. I seek to maintain the natural cycle of things. Yet when it comes to the design and maintenance of a garden, it is all too tempting to work against nature.

Man, by his very presence as the dominant specie on the planet, seeks to control everything around and beneath him. We do it without thinking. It's in our nature to exert our influence, either as help or oppression. We can see this in our gardens. Rarely are they entirely wild places. Even if we let them do their own thing, we're still likely to keep a boundary fence or hedge. We wish to tell the world that this is our patch, to do with as we will.

Robert Frost suggested that our actions are

complementary to that of Nature, and that we are merely putting the finishing touches to her work. "Nature does not complete things," he said. "She is chaotic. Man must finish, and he does so by making a garden and building a wall." But it is in the chaos, or in a mixture of chaos and order, where the best gardens (suited to the needs of wildlife and man) are to be found. As Penelope Hobhouse said, "Gardens are a collaboration between art and nature ... [but] Nature soon takes over if the gardener is absent."

The most valuable thing I learned during my landscape architecture degree was to study what grows naturally in an area. "Take a look in the woods, hedgerows and meadows near to your garden," I was taught. "Note the species of trees, shrubs, climbers, wildflowers, bulbs, ferns, mosses and grasses. Doing so enables us to not only know what will grow in our soil, but how to make our planting schemes appear naturalistic.

It was Ralph Waldo Emerson who wrote, "What is a weed? A plant whose virtues have not yet been discovered." I am of his school of thinking, often preferring wild flowers to ornamental ones. I like the idea of having a garden made up entirely of native species. I'd have hawthorn, field maple and holly growing in my hedges; dog roses and wild honeysuckle would clamber up trellises and over archways; cow parsley would fill my borders in spring; meadowsweet would scent my garden in summer; foxgloves would stand proud until autumn; my lawn would be filled with daisies, clover and buttercups; and moss would cover shady walls and paths. It would be a wild place, by my choosing.

Whether I could see my wildflower vision become reality remains in question. There are so many ornamental plants that have become good friends – such as Euphorbia characias 'Wulfenii', Hosta sieboldiana, Wisteria sinensis, Dicentra spectabilis, and Alchemilla mollis – that I would feel like an unloving parent if I didn't share my home with them. So a mixture of the two styles is more likely, with wild and naturalistic plants mingling with their ornamental cousins.

You'll notice that I got all Latin on you then. Apologies. It's just that when referring to friends, it's best to use their proper names rather than common ones. Look the plants up, by all means, but as Monty Don says, "You do not need to know anything about a plant to know that it is beautiful." Plants bring us pleasure. That's the main thing. But you'll eventually want to know more about them, I promise. You'll want to be able to recognise them at different times of year; know their preferences, idiosyncrasies, and family relatives, knowing them as a true friend would. As William Robinson wrote, "Do not pay too much attention to labelling. If a plant is not worth knowing, it is not worth growing."

While the concept of a totally wild garden might have romantic appeal, the appeal of it, over time, would soon wane. I've seen what it would become, and it isn't pretty. Back in 1991, when I was seventeen, I was asked to help an elderly gentleman 'get control' of his garden. It was to be half a day's work as a favour to a family friend. I arrived at the gentleman's house one afternoon, and was pleasantly surprised to be greeted by a neatly trimmed front lawn, rows of busy lizzies, and standard roses growing in the front garden. "Shouldn't be too much of a problem," I thought. "Twenty minutes and I'll be done."

I rang the doorbell and, after an age, heard the shuffling of footsteps in the hallway behind the door; then the rattling of security chains being removed, and finally the turning of a key in the lock. The door opened and there stood Bill, the gentleman, looking bright-eyed but frail.

"I've come to help with the garden, Bill," said I. "But it doesn't look too bad. Where do you need help?"

"Round the back," he replied, his face grimacing uncomfortably as he spoke. Come this way. I'll show you."

Bill walked me through his house until we reached the back door.

"I'll need your help to open the door," he whispered, as he handed me the key. I put the key in the lock and turned it. The mechanism opened instantly. I turned the handle of the door and pushed. And pushed. And pushed some more. It wouldn't move. I then put my shoulder against the door and gave it a serious shove. It moved. An inch. I thrust repeatedly, until, inch-by-inch, the door opened enough for me to squeeze through. And there, in the garden, I looked up, and up, towards a towering wall of blackthorn, bramble and nettles. It reached the height of the upstairs windows and allowed little light below.

"Er, Bill," said I, "When exactly did you last garden out here?"

"What, out the back?" he exclaimed, in complete puzzlement. "I've never set foot in this back garden. Never seen the need. I keep that front garden tidy, for sure, as it keeps the neighbours happy, but this back garden's always been full of weeds and junk. Ever since I moved here."

"When exactly was that?" I enquired, fearing the answer.

"1957," replied Bill. "Same year Aston Villa won the FA Cup."

"So you're telling me you want thirty-four years' worth of wilderness cleared in half a day? It's unlikely.

I can't even see into your garden, let alone work out the size of the task."

"Oh. Well if I remember correctly," said Bill, stroking his chin, "the garden stretches back to those Lombardy poplars over there."

"What?!" exclaimed I, and then made a noise like a high-pitched tuning fork. "They must be eighty yards away."

"Suppose so," said Bill, raising his eyebrows. "But that shouldn't be a problem to a young chap like you. So here's what we'll do. You get your tools, roll up your sleeves, and get cracking; and I'll be in the kitchen, making a cuppa."

Bill left me standing in the garden with my hands

on my head, wondering what to do. Blackthorn is menacing at the best of times, its thorns being viciously sharp. It may provide wonderful sloes in winter and flowers in early spring, but it provides cuts and curses for the rest of the year. It also suckers from the base, making it spread as a tangled mass of thorns and stems. Add to this a Medusa's hair of brambles clambering atop the blackthorn crown, and a stinging weave of nettles knitted throughout, and I was presented with the ultimate example of Nature saying, "Come and have a go, if you think you're hard enough." I returned to the front garden. There, on the drive, was my bicycle and rucksack. I grabbed the bag, removing the secateurs, loppers, billhook, bow saw, and leather gauntlet gloves, and returned to the scene of the challenge.

I knew from experience that the best way to tackle blackthorn is to cut it at the base and drag it out. But I had nowhere to drag it to. So I got onto my hands and knees and – using the loppers, billhook and saw – began carving a tunnel into the thicket. I sliced, sawed and slashed my way, cutting and then pushing aside the branches. They hung above the ground, supported by the mesh of limbs above. I inched forward on my knees and then, in an agonising flash of pain, felt a thorn pierce through the cartilage beneath my kneecap. I screamed in agony, and then noticed the patch of blood appearing though my trousers. The thorn had snapped clean from the branch, so I had no option but to remove my trousers (keeping my knee bent) and tease the spike from my flesh. I pulled down my trousers and then, with one eye closed and the other on my knee, I tweaked and nudged the thorn from my body. I held it aloft. There, covered in blood, was a thorn two inches long and as menacing as a dagger held to one's throat. Thankfully it was still intact. I threw the thorn to one side, pulled up my trousers, and hobbled forward, squatting down so to keep my bodyweight on my boots rather than my knees.

Three hours and sixty yards later, I hit something solid and immovable: a cast iron bath propped up against a rotten (but dry) sofa. Behind it was a small clearing, wide and high enough for me to stand up in without scratching my face or stinging my eyes. I rubbed my bruised and blood-soaked knee, and then cursed the evil thicket. While blackthorn flowers are beautiful, and their berries supremely tasty when infused with gin, this wall of thorns had proven nearly impossible to conquer. (As Fletcher Steele said, "Any healthy plant will develop shocking bad manners if left to itself.")

I'd had enough. I'd spent most of the time inching along a tunnel like the Viet Cong, fearing for my safety and knowing that, even if I made it out alive, I wouldn't get paid for my troubles. I looked at the foam cushions of the sofa, and had an idea. I reached into my pocket, removed a box of matches, struck a match and flicked it onto the sofa. The flame grew steadily and then, as the foam caught light, burned rapidly upwards and outwards. I grabbed my tools and crawled as quickly as possible back down the tunnel. When I reached the house, and looked back, I could see flames twenty feet high roaring up from the wiry stems of bramble. It crackled, spitted and hissed, and then I heard a loud 'clung' as the bath buckled in the heat. The wind was driving the flames away from the house and up against the poplars. Soon one of them was alight, and I heard a screaming coming from the end of the garden. A woman was hysterical, not for fear of her life or damage to the trees, but because of something far more domestic.

"You barsturd!" She cried. "Don't you know this is a smokeless zone? I've got my washing out!"

Bill, whose phone was now ringing off the hook, came outside to see what all the fuss was about. "Ohh," he said, with a smile. "You made it all the way back there, did you? Good job! Though I think you've had it with the neighbour."

"Yeah," I replied, sheepishly, "She doesn't sound too happy."

"Not to worry," said Bill, in an upbeat way. "It won't matter soon."

"What do you mean?" I enquired.

"I'm moving house next week; got myself a room in one of those comfy retirement places."

"So why did you want this mess sorting out?"

"Ah, well, yes, I was going to get round to that. I've sold the house to a young couple. Nice they are. Wouldn't be fair to expect them to have to tidy their new garden, would it? Terribly nasty stuff blackthorn. Wouldn't wish it on my enemies. Still, you're a professional. It wouldn't bother you one bit, would it?"

Bonus Chapter

VI

PRICKING OUT

"How fair is a garden amid the trials and passions of existence."

Benjamin Disraeli

It wasn't so much the caution from the police, or the firemen spraying water over the house, that bothered me. Rather it was the screams and insults from the woman at the end of the garden whose washing I'd dirtied. By the time I'd been taken indoors 'for a chat' with the police, Madame Pottymouth had shouted every obscenity imaginable. I was, as she put it, a "dim-witted shat-for-brains weed-pulling lowlife." Was she misinformed? Or had my actions led her to a correct description? Was setting light to a near-impenetrable jungle of dried scrub – while I was in it – a dim-witted thing to do? Probably. But she wasn't the one wondering if she'd ever walk again, or frustrated at the prospect of returning to finish the job. She didn't know that I was studying four A Levels and was applying to go to university. All she saw (or rather heard) was a labourer working in a garden who, admittedly (to the police, neighbours and local press), did a very silly thing.

Talk about prejudices and stereotypes? Nonetheless, her abusive language affected me. For the first time in my life, I felt ashamed of being a gardener.

Having a job that is also one's hobby, and which provides one's sense of identity, can be tricky. When things at work become tough, what does one do to relax? If one's passion reminds us of the thing that causes us stress, then do we end up loving it less? There are many professional gardeners whose garden at home is a total mess, simply because they can't face bringing their work back with them. I became like this. The 'great fire incident' had, ironically, doused my passion for the one thing that had previously been sacred and special. Gardening became a job, a nine-to-five existence. My clients' gardens suffered. They became held as if in trance, maintained as they were rather than nurtured into what they could be.

Mirabel Osler wrote, "There can be no other occupation like gardening in which, if you were to creep up on someone at their work, you would find them smiling." This is very true, but for a short time it didn't apply to me. At least until I became the one sneaking up on myself, and catching myself unawares.

It appears to me that as people get older, and take on more responsibility, so they feel the need to run quicker to do everything in the ever-reducing time they have left. Following the fire incident, I set out to prove that I could be more than just a gardener. I got certificates, diplomas, a masters' degree, progressively more senior jobs, and an unhealthy ego. I blurred through twelve years of my life until, during a moment

PRICKING OUT

of contemplation, I realised that my life was in such a spin that I was now facing myself head on. I was watching myself as a younger man, working his garden and smiling. The 'me of my past' was happy; the 'me of now' was not. I needed to rediscover the person I once was. The person who, through a love of gardens, had cultivated the foundations of everything I would become. It led me to The Priory, my quiet place amid the madness of the world, and to a special garden I'd not seen since childhood.

Foley Infants School, where I received my first education, backs onto a scout camp and a large area of woodland known as Kinver Edge. It was here, in the late nineteen-seventies, that I planted a secret garden. You wouldn't know it was there, as it's not exactly 'designed', but to me it was a place of dreams. It began as a rescue mission. I'd sympathised with the conkers being smashed to pieces by the bigger kids in school and so, in a heroic act, I collected up all the conkers I could find on the ground that morning. I put them into my satchel and carried them home after school, throwing them into the wood at Kinver Edge. Later I did the same with acorns and hazelnuts until I felt confident that I'd not only saved these seeds, but also had given them a new and better chance in life. By the following spring, I'd discovered the exhilarations of riding a bicycle and flying a kite, and had all but forgotten the trees I'd planted. They were left to grow unassisted, and anonymously.

It was during a dawn walk from my parents' house, twenty years later, that I decided to take a detour. I walked my old route to school, pausing at Kinver Edge and the scout camp, looking to see if the trees had grown. It was one of those 'I wonder?' moments that challenge us to see whether dreams of our past have materialised. I studied the hedgerows and woodland edges. There were areas that had been clipped, strimmed or cleared. Parts had grown wild and others looked the same as in my youth. While it was impossible to identify specific trees, there were plenty in the right age group – oaks with trunks approaching eight inches in diameter; hazels uncoppiced and bushy; but alas there were no horse chestnuts. Nature, it seemed, had allowed only the native seeds to grow. But what I felt, when walking alongside the wood, was that it was mine. I was proud to be there, having helped it become what it is today, and that I'd put my faith into the right things. My love of gardening may have waned temporarily, but everything I'd done before and since then was in support of the original dream. If nothing else, as I gazed up at the canopy of oak and hazel leaves, I knew that I'd regained my genuine and wholehearted love of gardening. If any aspect of my life needed pricking out and thinning so that other areas could flourish, it was not my love of gardening. It was the things I do under sufferance for others, which pay the bills but do not give me life. (Does this ring true with you? Are you, like me, a seedling who looks to the sky in search of something greater than you have – or are – today?) Whatever I did as my day job, or however I lived my life, I'd be able to garden once again as a way of balancing the pressures of living. As Chris Baines wrote, "Just a few minutes of quiet relaxation amongst trees, with bird song and bumblebees for entertainment, and even the most exhausted of city workers is ready of anything." I'd rediscovered the thing that most made me who I am. I'm a countryman, for sure; but really, deep down, I am a gardener. Nothing more. Nothing less.

I was reminded of this journey today when, after returning home from work, I decided to spend time in my garden and allow it to heal the wounds of a day at the office, where a simple gardener faces greater threats than blackthorns, bushfires and police interrogation.

The sun was high in the sky when I opened the door to my garden. As I had hoped, the nearside corner of the patio was in full sun. It invited me to sit there, and be joined by a glass of merlot for company. I accepted the invitation, pulling up a chair and sipping my wine. I rolled my head on my shoulders and let out a deep and satisfying groan. It is always good to be in the garden, especially on a warm May evening when the air is scented with the delicate perfume of Clematis montana, when swallows chatter and swoop overhead, and bumblebees buzz about the garden waiting for the lavenders to bloom. The garden is especially green at this time of year. (It's mostly green throughout the year, it being a north-facing garden that relies on foliage for interest.) The green-grey leaves of Alchemilla mollis and Aquilegia 'McKana Hybrids' gave a soft but cooling look to the borders. They contrasted the pale yellow-green leaves of Dicentra spectabilis alba and the emerging tubular spikes of Hosta fortunei 'Aurea'. Dryopteris felix-mas ferns proudly displayed their fronds in the shadiest corner of the garden, and shrub roses 'Geoff Hamilton' and 'Gertrude Jekyll' grew strongly but leggily alongside me.

The temptation with gardens is to always have an eye on plants that can be moved, trimmed, propagated, or planted. They lull us into 'a relaxed state of frenzy', where we may appear outwardly calm (often comatose) but inside we are pottering, plotting, and dreaming. Not so tonight. My wine was swiftly consumed and, as I sat with my face tilted to the sun, I could think of nothing but the tranquil beauty of a garden. Of how, in that moment, I was alive and in paradise. That gardening, even if we have no desire to pick up a trowel or fork, is a happy and healthy marriage of mind, body and place. It gives us purpose, an inner fire that fuels our dreams and encourages moments where we may relax and savour the results of our efforts. For this is what keeps us human in a progressively artificial, technological world. It is why and how we live.

May

VII

THE COTTAGE GARDEN

"How I would love to be transported into a scented Elizabethan garden with herbs and honeysuckles, a knot garden and roses clambering over a simple arbour."

Rosemary Verey

DANGER! Do not enter! So read the sign at the entrance to a half-acre patch of wasteland near my childhood home. The sign, erected by the owner of the local estate, was designed to deter trespassers, fly-tippers and adventurous schoolchildren from entering the area. It failed on all three counts. There was a well-trodden path across the site, a rusty old washing machine and fridge freezer discarded in the middle, and the six-foot high nettles that covered the ground were riddled with tunnels from endless games of hide-and-seek. I was one of the children who saw the overgrown and scrubby wilderness as an adventure playground. Sure, there was an open well and a deep brick-lined hole to be wary of, and lots of broken glass and unsteady rubble that caused frequent cuts and bruises. But they just added to the adrenaline and riskiness of being there. It was one of those places that presented endless opportunities for exploration and discovery. But then, as we kids grew up (and the younger children seemed less interested in doing anything outdoors), the forbidden area grew quiet and more heavily overgrown. It became lost beneath its own vegetation.

Eight years later, when enduring the lung burn of a school cross-country run, I found myself once again hiding amongst the nettles of the site. My classmates limped, wheezed and wobbled past, while I caught my breath and planned a detour to the bus stop. It was a clever move. Not because I could arrive at the finish line a clear ten minutes ahead of everyone else (and secure a place on the rostrum with the athletic – and somewhat 'forwardly-cushioned' – sports mistress) but because it altered my perception of my childhood playground.

I was only eight years old when I'd last been there. But now, aged sixteen (and having been a 'professional' gardener for five years) I began to notice different things. More specifically, I began to question things. Why, for example, was there a well in the middle of an overgrown patch of land? What was the big brick-lined hole in its centre? Why was there so much rubble? And why were nettles growing thicker and taller here than elsewhere?

As my classmates ran from view, I stood up and began to properly explore the area. I found a pile of rubble, and followed it in a clockwise direction. It formed a complete rectangle surrounding the hole in the ground. To its right was the old well. I walked over to it and peered down the shaft, seeing my reflection some thirty feet down. (Whatever would have happened if my friends or I had fallen down there?) True to the notice, this area

really was dangerous. And it was obvious that a building once stood here. A cottage of some description, with a cellar and its own water supply. I struggled to guess the age of the building, but from the thin handmade bricks and lime mortar, I estimated it to be well over a hundred years old. And from the accumulation of rubbish, extent of the weed growth, and size of the ash and elders growing up through the rubble, I calculated it to have been ruined for at least fifty years.

Hmm. A half-acre plot of land; a ruined cottage. What about the garden? Did one ever exist? And, more importantly, did any of it remain? I decided to return at the weekend, to take a proper look.

Saturday arrived and I cycled to the site of the old cottage. I'd brought a garden fork, a rake and a long-handled slasher with me. Being the gardener of the village, nobody would question my activities; they'd just assume that I'd been employed to tidy up the site. So I began clearing the nettles (and brambles, and elder, and dog rose, and grasses) from the area. Soon I could see the bones of a garden. The tangled remains of an apple and damson orchard grew at the far end of the site; to its right was an old vegetable garden (I could tell this from the sprawling carpet of horseradish and mint); alongside the rubble was a mound of box shrubs, assumedly either an old parterre or herb garden; in front of the cottage was mostly grass, honesty, and dog roses – possibly a lawn and border, and site of an old archway; to the left of the cottage was a hummock of soil, most likely an old compost heap; behind it grew the tallest nettles. I flattened them with the rake and exposed the soil. Sure enough, it was dark and charred: the site of a bonfire. I worked my way in a grid-like fashion across the site, pushing my fork into the ground every three feet, noting where the soil was soft and where it was hard, gritty or stiff. I drew a mental picture of location of borders, paving, gravel pathways, and lawns. The layout of the garden was surprisingly formal, with only straight lines to the paths and borders. This hinted at a garden with 1940s influence, when practicality and productiveness were (in my limited understanding) more important than sweeping design statements or relaxed use of space. So perhaps it hadn't been ruined for as long as I thought?

I imagined the gardener who once worked this soil. Was he or she an enthusiastic gardener? I'd say so by the size of the compost heap, though I'd have expected a skilled gardener to have returned the goodness to the borders and vegetable garden. So maybe they had to vacate the site prematurely? He or she was someone who made their land work for them. The entire site was cultivated and yet this green-fingered enthusiast still had time (and patience) to restrain the perpetual expansion of horseradish and mint. But it wasn't enough for me. I needed to know more about the gardener.

Where to start? I could have visited the library in search of electoral records or old photos; spoken to local residents or approached the estate owners. But gardening is a personal thing. Plants speak to us, and we to them. And a garden, in any state, contains clues that a gardener can most easily read. (Think of the structure of a hedge, for example. You can tell by the forking of the branches at what height and approximate frequency the hedge was cut.) Where then in this abandoned garden should I start to look? Where would tell me the most about the gardener who worked here? It was obvious: I would explore the compost heap and its immediate surroundings. This is the heart of a garden, where the cycle of life is most evident.

I set to work digging over the compost heap, and found nothing but soil and nettle roots. Then I began forking over the area at the rear of the pile, near to the bonfire area. I hit the jackpot. There, at the base of a hawthorn hedge, were the remains of a digging fork and hoe. Proper tools for someone not afraid of hard work.

A GARDENER'S YEAR

THE COTTAGE GARDEN

I dug deeper, bringing up pieces of shattered pottery and dozens of broken clay smoking pipes. And then, as I stood up and stretched my back, I noticed something unusual in the hedge. There, wedged within the fused branches of a hawthorn, was the curved blade of a pruning knife. Next to it was a blackened and moss-covered clay pipe, fully intact and placed as if ready to smoke. I felt my hands grip the garden fork and energy warm my muscles. Was this gardener here with me in spirit? Was he readying me to return his garden to its former glory? I glanced again at the pruning knife and clay pipe. They were at rest, remnants of what was. I felt like I was digging up a grave. For the first time ever, I felt uncomfortable in this place. My actions, of clearing the site and revealing its past, had not brought this garden back to life. Far from it. I realised that the garden had evolved into what it was meant to be: a playground for many, where children laughed and adults walked contentedly. All those formal lines had gone, buried beneath leafy informality; somewhere that made people smile and – regardless of warning signs – invited them in. That was the garden's great success, something that is so difficult to replicate. As Lawrence Halprin wrote, "The great challenge for the garden designer is not to make the garden look natural, but to make the garden so that the people in it will feel natural."

I gathered my tools, and walked away from the cottage garden, knowing that no amount of horticultural skill on my part could make the garden any better than it had looked earlier in the day, before I'd begun stripping it of its magic.

JUNE

VIII

A NAKED ASSAULT

"While it is not obligatory to dabble your bare feet in the dirt to get the most out of your garden, it is a pity not to go barefoot at some time."

Monty Don

Some advice for you: if ever you find yourself lying in the bath when your wife shouts "Cat! Shoo!" make sure that once you've jumped from the water, you grab a towel before you run downstairs and into the garden. And if you have a nosy neighbour as I do, who taps her windowpane whenever she disapproves of something you're doing in the garden, then don't just stand there, tackle out, looking up and waving (your hand) at her, pretending that what you're doing is normal. It's not. As I was reminded this evening when, after taking a break from protecting my garden from the poop-leaving moggie, I found myself back in the garden, feeling 'somewhat exposed'. Mrs Stroppup opened her bedroom window and shouted, "If you're going to play Adam and Eve, then at least have the decency to cover yourself with a fig leaf or, looking at it, an oak leaf – that ought to do the job. And keep that sort of naughtiness indoors. You're putting my cat off its essential business!"

Alas, there comes a time in a man's life when he realises that his manhood could be covered by not so much the fig leaf, as the fig itself. Cold weather or not, he's not the man he once was. Mrs Stroppup was right. I looked down and realised that I really was approaching 40, and that my fruit had been left withering too long on the branch. I lowered my head in shame and returned indoors, to the confidence-boosting warmth of the bath.

Now that I've shared my naked self with you, it's time for me to make an honest announcement: that Fennel, after thirty-five years of gardening, has gone properly organic. No longer will my roses be sprayed each week, or my fruit canes fed with sulphate of ammonia; incendiary devices have been removed from around my carrots and cabbages, and Keith the scarecrow's plastic anorak is gone. I, and my garden, have gone au naturel.

I am informed by my *Experts' Guide to Not Spraying the Hell out of Your Garden and Instead Sitting Back and Watching Your Plants Turn to a Festering Mass of Black Spot, Aphids and Rust, While Getting Some Tasty Vegetables in the Process* that the secret to organic gardening is to make your garden as wildlife-friendly as possible, avoiding monocultures and overly fertilised (lush) plants, and that companion planting (with plants such as marigolds, garlic and nasturtiums) can deter, or lure, pests from your more valuable crops. That thriftiness and recycling is central to keeping the goodness in your garden. Waste not, want not. And when your compost heap is overflowing with potato peelings, and your

A NAKED ASSAULT

chicken run is filled with cabbage leaves, you can take a casual walk down the garden, drop your trousers, and pee in a watering can. This natural urea can be diluted five parts water to one part wee and sprinkled directly onto your plants, or into your compost heap. Talk about organic gardening taking the pee? It sounds gross, but it works a treat. In my seventeen years as a garden labourer, I never once asked to go to the toilet. (Just don't try this technique on indoor plants, as it can make your conservatory pong like a tramp's trousers.)

Ultimately, for organic gardening to work, it has to be part of a holistic approach. There's no point having an organic vegetable patch when you're spraying other areas of the garden. Spores, pests and their predators live and feed throughout the garden. So if you're not absolute in your commitment to organics, then all you're doing is keeping a tidy front room when the rest of your house is in shambles. And you have to be patient. Seeing the results of your switch can take up to three years (certainly in the case of organic manures, which first have to condition the soil before they feed your plants). But that doesn't mean we have to stand idly by whenever aphids, caterpillars and slugs are munching our plants. We can get manual, protecting our plants with netting or fleece, or rubbing aphids from the growing tips, picking caterpillars from our cabbages and squishing them or feeding them to the chickens; slugs and snails can be squashed when seen, or drowned in jam jars full of beer. (Best way to go, if you ask me.) Predators – such as ladybirds, lacewings, birds, and hedgehogs – should be encouraged into the garden by keeping some areas untidy. (It's easier for a predator to feed on its doorstep than have to 'go out' for lunch.) And we can place matting around our carrots to avoid cabbage root fly, and wrap grease bands around our apple trees to avoid damage from wingless moths. It requires more work and proactivity, but you have the reassurance of knowing that you're doing the right thing, especially when you taste the difference between organic and chemically reared fruit and vegetables. (I once ulcerated my lips by eating a carrot straight from a farm field; such was the concentration of chemicals on it.) And when we have children, and notice the ratio of their size to that of the food they eat, we can see how easily they would be affected by what they consume. (We're aware of their behavioural changes whenever they consume sugary drinks or E Numbers, but what about chemical fertilisers and pesticides? How quickly, and in what way, would they be affected? All it would take is a child crying, "Mummy, my tummy and head hurts" for us to ring the ambulance, clear the larder, and empty the garden shed of anything unnatural.)

My friend John (sadly no longer with us, but whom you will read about later) was a farmer and gardener throughout his eighty-three years. I remember him telling me of his experiences after the war, when farmers were encouraged to grow intensively using chemical fertilisers. "T'was the first time we'd done it," he said, as he rubbed his fingertips. "Seemed daft at the time, what with all the slurry produced by the pigs, but it was the thing to do. So we opened up the bags, scooped up the white powder with our hands, and transferred it to the hopper at the back of the tractor. We then set to work, broadcasting the fields. The harvests were impressive, and we ended up spreading the pig muck on the pastureland instead. Didn't think any more about it until 1995 when, during a hot summer, all my fingernails and toenails fell out. I saw the doctor, who sent some of my nails off for tests. The results came back saying 'high concentration of ammonium nitrate'. It seems that my body had absorbed the chemicals and, over a period of fifty years, had slowly pushed them to the extremities of my fingers and toes until, during a particularly warm season, my fingernails dropped out while I was tying in some raspberry canes." John held up his hands, and I saw the yellow stubs of fingernails that were left. "They never really grew back," he said, as he flicked his thumb against his index finger. "But do you know, if you go up to the fields at the back of the farm, where we grazed the cattle, the grass there is lusher than anywhere else in these parts. It just goes to show the value of good honest muck."

Honesty, therefore, is the way forward when it comes to growing food for the table. It's what I've been reminded of today, and what I shall ambassador henceforth. We are, after all, people of the earth; here because of everything that's around us. So let's not bugger it all up for others, or us or tip the delicate balance of nature. Because if we do, we know who'll be looking down and pointing a nail-less finger at us. It won't be Mrs Stroppup, or The Great Creator, but someone who worked the land for over seventy years and knew what it meant to be organic.

And as for my neighbour? I don't need to prove anything to her. She knows what I am, and what I've got. I've laid it bare for her to see. But what do I care? I've got my plants, I feel good about being organic, and I have built a closer relationship with you through my openness. I feel humbled, which is how gardening encourages us to be. As Joanne R Barwick wrote, "There's little risk of becoming overly proud of one's garden because gardening by its very nature is humbling. It has a way of keeping you on your knees."

JULY

IX

URBAN GREENERY

"Suburbia is where the developer bulldozes out the trees, then names the streets after them."

Bill Vaughan

"Ruddy weeds!" shouted my neighbour as he pulled, tugged and thrashed at every green thing in his garden. "Whoever heard of glossy leaved blue flowering weeds, anyway?" he bleated. "Things that sprawl over everything and make my garden look like a jungle on Mars? They've gotta go. Bleedin' nature-infested bushes. Just look at all these bugs!"

"I think you'll find," said I, peering over the fence that separates our gardens, "that the weeds are actually ornamental plants called ceanothus, and that the bugs are friendly lacewings."

"Uh?" He replied, as he looked up, frowning.

"The builders planted the shrubs before you moved in." I continued. "They're not weeds. And those green-winged insects are eating the aphids that are living on the plants."

"Don't care!" snarled my neighbour, as he ripped the roots of the ceanothus from the ground. "All plants are weeds and all bugs are vermin! I'm paving over the lot, so that I won't ever have to come out here again and miss another minute of Match of the Day. I hate this place. Why we ever moved from the city, to a house with a garden, I shall never know!"

I retreated behind the fence, and slumped with sadness knowing that someone could detest having a garden. I'd heard about people who poisoned their borders with engine oil, or drenched their gardens with residual herbicide; and once, when working at the garden centre, I sold a propane-powered flamethrower to a man whose garden was infested with couch grass and ground elder (not that it would have done much good; the strength of these weeds is in their roots). But I'd not experienced such behaviour first hand.

When I think of plants, I hear the words of Martin Luther King, who said, "For in the true nature of things, if we rightly consider, every green tree is far more glorious than if it were made of gold and silver." So when it comes to people who hate or abuse their garden, I passionately agree with Thomas Moore who said, "The soul cannot thrive in the absence of a garden. If you don't want paradise, you are not human; and if you are not human you don't have a soul."

Gardening is the most soulful thing we can do. Our gardens, like young children, ask for nothing more than to love and be loved. If we want to live and be real, then all we need do is sit in our garden, take interest, and be ourselves.

My neighbour had no interest in his garden, though he was characteristically being himself. My sadness

turned to anger as I heard the creaking and snapping of branches, though I knew I wouldn't act to defend the plants. Instead, a man in a red football top, who saw them as evil invaders, had sealed their fate.

Within a week, my neighbour's garden was covered in gravel and crudely laid paving slabs. By the look of the mess caused in the garden (soil was splashed up the fence panels and gravel was left scattered over the slabs), I concluded that he'd laid them in a hurry on a wet day, and that he hadn't laid any permeable membrane underneath. The slabs were sinking miserably into a quagmire of mud and contempt.

A GARDENER'S YEAR

George Herbert said, "Love your neighbour, yet pull not down your hedge." It proves that good hedges and fences make good neighbours, giving us the option of whether we have to speak to them. Mrs H and I have mostly harmless neighbours (though 'John Daniels' at number 56 acts a bit strange when he's had too much whisky) and, all things being even, we probably look and behave a bit odd to them. They're the ones who draw the short straw each morning as I clip-and-clop past their houses in my hobnail boots, and insist upon making the largest snowman in the Northern Hemisphere each winter. (It stands proud, with crossed arms, in the middle of the road, stopping anyone from driving to work.) And I'm the only person on our estate with a brazier in their garden, who is confident enough to fill it with waste paper and oily rags and set light to it on a windy day. (I've only lost one fence panel in the process, but that's a different story.) I am, I admit, eccentric. But life would be very dull if we were normal, boring and conforming, would it not? Best we spice it up a bit with some erratic and individual behaviour.

Which is why, last Saturday morning, when my neighbour and his wife were out shopping, I took a sneaky look over the fence at the work he'd done. It really was a mess. Not only were the slabs poorly laid, and the gravel unraked, but all the shrubs, turf and perennials were piled up against his garden shed. He'd paved around this funeral pile, not having any intention of taking the plants to the tip, or finishing the job properly. Within months, the vegetation – and side of his shed – would have rotted down and he'd have a brown stinking mess to contend with. But this was only the half of it. As I looked left, back towards the house, I saw a line of builder's pallets propped up and forming a makeshift fence across his garden. Behind it was a sea of empty beer cans and bottles, brimming to the top of the pallets. There were thousands of them, assumedly thrown from the house and stashed there in an 'out-of-sight, out-of-mind' way. The garden was just a dumping ground. I could only assume that my neighbour's intention was to keep moving the pallets back until his whole garden was covered in rubbish.

How could a pile of waist-deep bottles and cans be more appealing than flowering plants? Perhaps that wasn't my neighbour's intention? Maybe, by dumping his litter in the garden, he was burying any memory of it? His actions were working, but in doing so he was showing his slobbish side to the world – and upsetting his neighbour.

I folded and placed my arms on the fence, and rested my head upon them, looking down at the slabs in the garden below. There, in a crack between the paving, were the leaves of a dandelion growing defiantly against my neighbour's wishes. Something in his garden had survived. I tipped my hat at the little plant. If it had been growing in my garden then it would certainly have ended up as rabbit food, but in his? It was spectacular. I prayed that it would continue to grow unnoticed, so that it could flower and set seed. And then I had an idea. I had a box of grass seed in the shed. My neighbour was out. And the wind was blowing towards his garden...

I fetched a pair of stepladders and positioned them

against the garden fence. I grabbed the box of seed from the shed, climbed the ladders and flamboyantly flung handfuls of grass seed over his garden. It settled in all the cracks in the pavement, in amongst the gravel, up against his fence and shed, and between the bottles and cans. I kept going until the three-kilo box was empty. Then (in for a penny, in for a pound) I fetched the hosepipe and sprinkler and soaked his garden. When I was done, I went indoors and booked a last-minute holiday to Wales. Mrs H and I grabbed our stuff and left quickly.

We returned, two weeks later, to see our neighbour's garden awash with green and him and his wife standing amongst the bottles in their garden, scratching their heads. My neighbour's wife was speaking to him in a stressed tone of voice. "I told you this would happen," she shrieked. "You bodged laying those slabs, didn't you? Because you wanted to get back inside and watch Manchester United on the television. Well I've had enough. Either we go back to the city, or the television goes!"

My neighbour turned to his wife and, holding her hand, said, "I'll call the estate agent first thing tomorrow morning. And don't worry, I'll get this garden cleared up before the 3pm kick-off."

August

X

DUST AND DESIRE

The height of summer is here. Barbecues are lit, paddling pools are filled, and parasols are erected. The sun is blazing down and the sky has been cloudless for weeks. People are outside in their gardens, laughing, playing, eating, drinking, and sunbathing. They are oblivious to the slowing of growth and browning of leaves that occurs in this heat. Whether gardeners or not, they are right to be outdoors, in their gardens and enjoying life. As James Dent said, "A perfect summer day is when the sun is shining, the breeze is blowing, the birds are singing, and the lawn mower is broken." But I am sad. Still reeling from the shock of what my neighbour did to his garden last month, I am yearning to grow more plants, to compensate for those that lost their lives in the massacre. But I can't, not yet. It would be unwise to do so, because we have a hosepipe ban. Too many executives, it seems, washed too many cars on too many Sunday afternoons. Our reservoirs are critically low and our executives, driving about in their dusty BMWs, are seriously pissed off. So even if I did put some plants into the ground, I would be unable to water them. They would dry and wither, and remind me even more of my desire to see my garden overflowing with flowering things. (Of course, I should be smart about this and collect my cooled bathwater and then pour it onto the garden once the sun has set. The soap would act as a pesticide, the plants would get a good drink, and the soil would smell of Coconut Melba bubble bath. But I'm already in enough trouble with my neighbours. Accusations of 'nocturnal plant washing' are not what I need right now. So I shall continue mulching my roses with tealeaves, praying for rain, and sprinkling a forbidden can of water when nobody's looking.)

A garden needs water. Although mature plants will usually be able to fend for themselves, anything in pots, baskets or trays, or recently planted, will need careful and consistent application of the wet stuff. (It's a bit like sitting at a bar. If you stay there long enough, someone will buy you a drink, but if you've just arrived, you have to ask to be served.)

Back in 1995, when I worked at Rooksnest Estate, we experienced a drought like the one this year. Derek the Head Gardener decided that both the plants and his staff needed helping through the heat. He changed our working hours so that we wouldn't have to endure the heat of day. He'd arrive outside my cottage at 5am, three hours earlier than usual, driving the farm tractor and revving its engine until he saw me at the window. I'd then get dressed, exit my cottage, and jump aboard a trailer being pulled by the tractor. We'd then collect the other gardeners and be working by 5.15am. We'd undertake our duties until 1pm, when we'd break for the afternoon. We'd return to work at 6pm and, Woking in the shade of the house, would water non-stop for the three hours. Such is the luxury of working on an estate with its own borehole and a relaxed workforce who'd never heard of 'time-and-a-half' overtime pay.

Alas, my garden lacks the luxuries of Rooksnest. I don't have a borehole (only a football bore who lives next door), and it's just me in the garden. I guess this makes me my own head gardener, and that I can decide how, where, and when I will garden? Strangely, this was never my ambition. While I hold all gardeners, and especially head gardeners, with utmost respect, I never saw myself as the one wearing the head gardener's bowler hat. I was always lured away by my artistic temperament, keen to express my creativity by designing gardens more than caring for them. This paid better and honed my skills at understanding client needs (which led to jobs in marketing and business management), but I wish I'd spent more years working on estates, broadening my experience both in gardening and estate management.

Recently I was approached to work for a company setting up business in a middle-eastern country. The salary on offer was outrageous (it would have made me a millionaire within two years), but the role would have required me to be away from my family for six months at a time (returning for a meagre two weeks per year). The recruitment head-hunter, speaking on the telephone, said, "It's the chance of a lifetime! You alone are my shortlist for the job. Go for the interview. They'll cover your travel costs. Though obviously you'd need to consider the political climate out there. It is..." she paused for a couple of seconds, "...somewhat unsettled."

I have a question: if you were in this situation, what would you do? Would you go for the interview? Would you conduct it over the phone? Would you hold out and ask for more money? Would you speak to your family? Would you accept, or politely decline the offer of employment?

Before I could respond, the recruitment agent added, "Just out of interest, and in case the money's not enough, what figure would you accept?"

I paused, considering her question, and then felt a smile form on my lips. "I am not for sale," I said, chuckling. "Quality of life is priceless, so no amount of money could persuade me to sacrifice everything I hold dear. The job would be a fabulous opportunity for

someone, of that I'm sure, but you're speaking to the wrong man." I thanked the agent for contacting me, and then said farewell, feeling my heart race as I put down the receiver.

My attitude to work had, during the course of the phone call, come full circle since my time since Rooksnest. In the eighteen years since I'd worked on the estate, my priorities had changed from seeking an ever-heavier curriculum vitae and paycheque, to one that catered principally for the needs of my family (both their need for me, and mine for them) and for my expectations regarding quality of life. I am a father and husband; an all-round countryman; I walk the fields, woods and rivers, studying the natural history of what

I find; I fish and shoot in season; I tend to my garden; and I write about my adventures. These activities define me. They are my raison d'être. Without them, I would cease to live. So the thought of putting my life, and that of my family, on hold for two years (while I suffered the isolation, burning sand, and barren landscape of a desert country) was too much to bear. It would never happen. If my career activities since my time at Rooksnest were a javelin, travelling quickly and allowing me to see things from a great height, then that spear had come to an abrupt landing during the phone call with the head-hunter. Sure, I might pick it up and throw it in another direction, but not towards money at the cost of everything else. There's only so much we need in order to live, after which it's our choice of how much living we trade in return for those round pieces of metal and crumpled sheets of paper.

Wouldn't it be nice to think of a career in life, rather than a career at work? Where soil on our fingers replaces coins in our pockets, and personal identity replaces a job title. Where we measure success by the amount of free time we own, redeeming it in exchange for doing the things we most enjoy. It's a nice thought, but sometimes we just have to 'be' in the moment and not plan a contrived life. (If everything were in our control, planned and 'executed' efficiently, then we'd be dead. There'd be no opportunity for free thinking, radical behaviour, or the intrigue of receiving an unexpected Valentine's Day card.) So no. This is not the best way to be. As George Harrison said, "I'm not really a career person. I'm a gardener, basically."

Well said, George. After all, you were the one whose guitar gently wept.

Which brings me back to today. The heat outside is unbearable. Still, it is nearly thirty degrees cooler than if I were in that middle-eastern country. So I am going back to my roots. I'm going to follow Derek's advice and take the afternoon off. I shall sit in the cool of my study, sipping an iced Gin & Tonic, and dream about rain. As Monty Don wrote, "The one smell that is more heartachingly beautiful than the scent of any plant, and impossible to capture or contain within a garden, is the smell of warm dusty soil immediately after a light shower of rain." I am imagining that scent right now. A billion imaginary droplets of heaven are landing upon the garden. And I am here, waiting for Mrs H and a Little Lady to return home; I am gazing upon my garden, sipping my drink, and not working. In fact, I'm doing all the priceless things that, at this exact moment in time, I most desire.

September

XI

THE SIZE OF ONE'S CARROT

"Let each good thing be so bold and so well grown as to make its presence felt."

William Robinson

"It's not the size of one's carrot," said I to a crowd of onlookers, "but its firmness in the hand after a good tug – from the soil." It was quite possibly the most inappropriate thing I'd ever said. I was at the time receiving a 'Highly Commended' award at the BBC Gardeners' World Live show at the National Exhibition Centre. I had a certificate in one hand and, with the other, was shaking that of Susan Hampshire, famous actor and the VIP Guest invited to present awards at the show. I was the fresh-faced young garden designer who'd impressed the judges but couldn't think of anything better to say when presented with my award. As I stood there, being photographed by the national press and holding the hand of the woman who played Fleur in The Forsyte Saga, all I could think of was 'didn't she get naked in the film Malpertuis?' and, 'I wonder if she, the mature woman that she is, might respond to some of my youthful charm?' Alas, she did not.

She was completely professional and dignified, and instead asked me about the lilies I had on display next to my designs.

"These look and smell magnificent," she said, as she tried to let go of my hand, "how do you stop them from wilting under the exhibition lights?"

"Iced water in the vase," I replied. "Contrary to popular belief, a cold shower doesn't affect the firmness of a stem, so long as your stock has endless stamina."

"Oh, I see," she replied, through a forced smile. "It sounds effective, though it appears one of your ice cubes has melted?" She glanced down, raised her perfect eyebrows, and smirked.

When the presentation was over, and everyone had departed, I looked down, wondering what she'd seen. There, on my left trouser leg, was one of those damp patches that proved the rule that 'no matter how much you shake your peg, there's always a drop that gets your leg.' Trust me to go to the loo moments before meeting a screen siren. Still, I still had my lilies, and a vase of incredibly cold water.

It's amazing what we can say when put under pressure, when we lose all sense of appropriateness. Like the man who, when in court for a serious traffic offence, said to the judge, "Your Honour, you must understand that I had been driving for twenty years before I fell asleep at the wheel." Or the male streaker who, when arrested, asked the policeman, "Is your hat waterproof?"

I remember, back in 2005, going for a lunchtime business meeting at the Department for Environment,

THE SIZE OF ONE'S CARROT

Food and Rural Affairs (Defra). After I'd walked past the Houses of Parliament, into the Government offices, through the tubular glass x-ray machines, along the marble corridors and into the oak-panelled offices of the Environment Minister (who was out, so his offices were being used for meetings), I was quaking and wishing that I'd not worn my wax jacket. A man in a three-piece pin stripe suit, who stood tall and had all the pride of a man about to be knighted, greeted me. He spoke with impeccable accent, asking, "My dear fellow, could I tempt you to a cop of teee, cooofeee or – something from the decaaarnter tray?" I stood there, in complete disbelief of my situation, and said, "Er, I used a sunbed once. Burned by bum something terrible. Couldn't sit down for ages. Car seats were out, bike saddle was impossible. But those padded leather chairs over there look very comfortable indeed." "Ah," he replied, chin held high, "I see that you're a brandy man, and have started early…"

You'd have thought that I'd have learned from all this. But, as I have found out today, I have not. Today, at work, I was summoned to a meeting with one of our top accounts. The customer had complained about the behaviour of a member of my team. I, being the manager, had to visit the client to apologise. I put three exercise books down the back of my trousers, got the train into London, and walked nervously (and somewhat uncomfortably) to the customer offices. By the time I arrived at the 14th floor, the client (a woman in her mid-forties) was pacing up and down and shouting at the thirty-or-so members of her team.

I entered the office and, as soon as I was announced, the client span round, pointed at me, and shouted, "YOU!" The office fell silent. Everyone's gaze turned to me, and, if I was not mistaken, the sound of a mouse riding a small Harley Davidson motorbike was heard coming from the back of my trousers.

The client, holding her arm out and pointing at me, began marching in my direction. I had ten seconds to think of something to say. Having no game plan or prepared script, I resorted to natural charm. I changed my pose to relaxed swagger, raised one side of my mouth, put a hand on my hip and then, when she halted just three feet from me, I said, "Hey, you're looking gooood, considering..."

"Considering what?!" she shouted.

"Considering your condition." I replied, smoothly. I leant forward and said, "I notice you've put on a significant amount of weight and are very emotional. So now you have the attention of the whole office, why don't you tell us your good news? You've got to be due...imminently."

The woman's mouth fell open. Someone dropped a pen, and the sound of an ambulance was heard outside.

"I – AM – NOT – PREGNANT!" Shouted the client, as she span in a full circle and snarled at her team. "I'm just FAT! Okay?!"

Not surprisingly, the charm that had never worked for me in the past did not work for me today. I was ordered to leave the building and instructed to send a written apology. For some reason, the client seemed in a worse mood when I left than when I arrived.

THE SIZE OF ONE'S CARROT

Still, I'd escaped a beating and deflected the woman's fury from her team. But I did wonder whether some of it was my fault?

You might be wondering what all this has to do with gardening? Well, there's a simple message in these stories: that when we have the opportunity for action, the best thing to do is nothing. At least until we have a clear and rational plan. It's too easy to go ploughing into a garden, for example, when you move into a new house. You're likely to enforce the wrong things, in the wrong places, without really knowing your garden.

Do not think of a garden as a blank canvas, onto which you can throw a Jackson Pollock.

A garden is something with character, with many nuances that are independent of the whims and necessities of its owner. It is far better to live in a garden for a number of years, without doing anything, than to 'transform' it on day one. While you might have a plan in your head, it will inevitably mature once you begin to listen to the garden.

Gardens, if you are not aware, talk to the gardener. A plant, for example, might look slightly under the weather, with yellowing leaves. The gardener, hearing the call, knows that something in the soil is wrong; it might be waterlogged, or short of nutrients, or containing pests that are eating the roots of the plant. Then there are those areas of the garden that, when you walk around your plot, just feel right. They might be sunny or sheltered spots that call out to be somewhere in which you should sit. Or you might notice, rather subtly, a favourite view within the garden that could be emphasised; or a boring view that calls out for the introduction of a focal point. Ultimately, how do you know how you will use the garden? You might have great plans for ornate borders, but do you have the time to maintain them? How much paved area do you need for entertaining? How much lawned area is needed for children or pets to play? Is digging up your whole garden for vegetables really the right solution when you could have an allotment down the road? The list is almost endless, but the message remains. Take your time in the garden. Listen to what it's telling you. And don't act until your script is clear in your head. You never know, the garden might give you some ideas you hadn't considered?

And please, when you meet the garden of your dreams, be polite and presentable. No carrot jokes, no melted ice cubes, no sun beds, and no comments about whether it's gained weight. You're together for the long run; and you should know better.

October

XII

GARDENER FOR HIRE

"The best way to garden is to put on a wide-brimmed straw hat and some old clothes. And with a hoe in one hand and a cold drink in the other, tell somebody else where to dig."

Tex Bix Bender

Mr and Mrs Gardner, of The Old Rectory, Worcestershire, had the most inappropriate surname of any couple who'd ever owned a garden. As accountants in the city, they had amassed a fortune saving the pennies of big businesses. They sought to display their wealth by purchasing a derelict property in the country and restoring it to its former glory. Which they did. In four months. When I arrived on site, as their newly appointed garden designer, they had more craftsmen working on site than would be found building your average football stadium. There was activity everywhere, with shouting and swearing going on in every room as builders, plasterers, carpenters, electricians, plumbers, painters, French polishers, carpet fitters, and a short Polish chap named Lucatz (who carried a spanner but didn't appear to be doing anything) all clambered over one another in an attempt to get everything done in record speed. The results were spectacular, if a little rushed. But what money wants, money gets. (The Gardner's bought a shell of a property, with no roof, windows, or floorboards, in August, and were on track to move into a completed house at Christmas. All that remained was for me to design and landscape the garden.)

The garden surrounding the Gardner's property consisted of two-acres of topiary (heavily overgrown and requiring some major tree surgery); a half-acre walled garden (walls intact, but the vegetables had seen what was coming and had gone to market); three acres of lawns (read 'ungrazed meadow'); a two-hundred-yard herbaceous border (filled mostly with ground elder and brambles); a formal terrace and parterre; a small orangery; and, as the property was next to a church, a quarter-acre graveyard (assumedly containing some rather restless occupants).

I sat down for my consultation meeting with Mr and Mrs Gardner on the 4th December, beginning with my usual pitch that focused on my desire to keep the garden authentic for the age and type of property, but ultimately it must fulfil the needs and aspirations of the client.

"Good. Just what we want to hear," said Mrs Gardner, as she stared at a swatch of curtain fabric. "So you'll be able to return the property to exactly how it looked in 1827, maybe 1828, but definitely not as late as 1830?"

"Erm, sure," I stuttered, quickly trying to think about whether an herbaceous border of that size and length was consistent with the period, or if they wanted to keep the dilapidated aluminium greenhouse in the vegetable garden.

"Excellent. Because, for your information, 1830 was when the house fell into disrepair. We don't want to be reminded of failure. We only accept success. And we expect results. Quickly! So am I right in assuming that you'll have the garden finished by New Year?"

"That's three weeks from now!" I exclaimed. "But I suppose it depends upon your budget, your specification, and what you mean by 'finished'."

"Isn't it obvious?" replied Mrs Gardner, as she threw the fabric swatch on the floor. "We have brought you in because you specialise in this sort of thing. The garden is already designed. We just want you to sort out what's there and replant what's not."

"And we know what's possible," said Mr Gardner. "We've seen those Alan Titchmarsh programmes. This sort of thing can be done in a day. So, giving you three weeks is most generous."

"Though obviously," interrupted Mrs Gardner, "we wouldn't hold it against you if you chose not to work on Christmas Day. So long as it's reflected in your price."

"Yes," said Mr Gardner, as he placed his hands on the table and leant back in his chair. "And we don't want any of those high maintenance plants, either. We've read that plants these days are bred so that they can be sprayed with a chemical that kills all other plants except the ones we want to keep. We want those sort of plants."

"I think you'll find," said I, through clenched teeth, "that those are cereal crops genetically modified by agrochemical companies so that they are unaffected by a given brand of herbicide. Do you really want me to plant wheat and barley in your borders? That's hardly authentic."

"Okay," replied Mr Gardner, who'd realised his mistake. "I'll accept your guidance on what plants to include, provided they're all fully grown. We can't be doing with any of that 'waiting for them to grow' nonsense."

"Absolutely!" stressed Mrs Gardner. "Especially the climbers. We want this house covered in lush flowering foliage when our guests arrive in January. We're having a house-warming party and we absolutely want them to smell roses and carnations and 'lawn things' growing outside their bedroom windows. If needed, speak to one of the carpet fitters who I'm sure will be able to supply climbers ready-grown on a roll. We don't care where you get them from, so long as they're here and rolled up our house in time for New Year."

"Same applies for the vegetable garden," added Mr Gardner. "We want to see it overflowing with melons and pineapples and grapes and cherries and-what was that vegetable you liked the other day dear?"

"Kumquats!" shouted Mrs Gardner, as if reprimanding her children for lagging behind. "And those yellow things you get as garnish on your dessert in fancy restaurants. I want lots of those. All grown neatly in rows and labelled with little copper tags."

"Oooohkaaaay" I said, wondering whether it was time for their medication. "You do know that most plants are dormant in December, and that most perennials

won't have any leaves right now."

"Get them imported!" shouted Mrs Gardner. "It's summer in Australia. They ought to have some leafy plants there. Like gum trees or something?"

"Sounds like your deadline is more important than your budget?" said I, going in for the kill.

"Absolutely," replied Mr Gardner. "If needs be, we see no problem in assigning up to two thousand pounds to this project."

Two thousand pounds? Surely that was less than they'd spent making cups of tea for the workmen on site?

I breathed deeply, then said, "Don't you mean two *hundred* thousand pounds?"

The Guinness Book of Records states that on the 4th December 1997, the sound of a gulp was heard four thousand miles from its point of origin. What it doesn't tell you is that the noise originated from the living room of a rectory in Worcestershire and was immediately followed by a phone call to the BBC, complaining that one of their programmes had caused a couple of property developers to feel like a right pair of wobbly Dimmocks.

I allowed the Gardner's time to compose themselves, and then explained that their budget would barely cover the cost of tree surgery for the topiary garden.

I emphasised that the average cost of a landscaping project, including design, labour and materials, was £140 per square metre; and that, once restored, a seven acre garden of their intended standard would most likely require a full-time gardener on a salary of circa £15,000 per year.

Eventually Mr Gardner's left eye stopped twitching and he was able to mutter the word "Yaar-eye-reckon-we-do." I talked Mr and Mrs Gardner through their options, and we agreed that I would do the bare minimum – a simple tidy-up of the garden to make it look presentable for their guests. I'd hire a ride-on mower to sort out the lawns, a hedge cutter to 'afro' the topiary and tidy up the parterre, a brush cutter to clear the herbaceous border and a rotovator to turn over the veg plot. And if I got it all done by Christmas, I'd secure the planting contract in the spring. It was a good deal. A million miles from their original intention, but certainly within their stated budget.

Did I achieve it? Yes I did. It was 'services rendered'. But the house was a different story. Lucatz finally figured out what to do with that spanner, and flooded the house. Just in time for Christmas.

NOVEMBER

XIII

THE GOOD LIFE

"Now I see the secret of making the best persons. It is to grow in the open air, and to eat and sleep with the earth."
Walt Whitman

Gardening is, by and large, a healthy and health-giving activity. Sure, there are plenty of risks posed by using machinery, sprays, knifes, secateurs, ladders, spades, wheelbarrows, or coming into contact with any plant that could prick, scratch, bruise, or bring us out in a rash. Not to mention the risk of drowning in a pond, or anaphylactic shock from being stung by a bee, or getting sunburned, or electrocuted, or poisoned; or being punched by a neighbour for growing the wrong sort of hedge. Yep. Like I said, gardening is a healthy thing to do. There are upsides. Like being outdoors in the fresh air, getting gentle exercise, feeling the parental joy of seeing something flower, or eating fresh vegetables straight from the garden. Keep this in your mind, because I want to highlight just how good gardening is for us physically and spiritually.

I know better than most what it is like to exist at both ends of the work/life spectrum. I worked in horticulture, either part-time or full-time, for 17 years. I was rarely ill during this time. I hardly suffered from colds or flu, even though I worked outdoors in all weathers. I've since held a variety of senior business management roles, where I have worked indoors, in a stuffy office, acutely feeling the pressures of corporate life. During the past ten years I have suffered regularly from coughs and colds, have taken a total of seven months off work with stress, have had shingles five times, have exhausted my adrenal gland three times (each time resulting in a week-long state of inertia), have suffered from depression (usually following periods of high creativity) and, soon after my career change, endured a breakdown that ended my life as I knew it.

I've experienced the lowest lows and the highest highs. And as I get older, I'm reminded more and more each day that a fast-paced work environment is not healthy. It ages us quicker by the week. Instead, it's the 'slowly slowly' approach that gets more done in the long run. A relaxed, quiet life is healthier, more sustainable, and kinder to oneself and those around us, especially when we spend as much time as possible outdoors, in our garden.

Writing these Journals is what helps me to keep the balance. They are the continuation of a promise I made many years ago, to know and be myself, to maintain a quality life, living it on my terms and sharing it with you as an honest representation of a person who is very real.

Mrs H and I spoke about this promise the other day, probing those areas of our life that could be better.

THE GOOD LIFE

While we are happy, and looking forward to moving to a greener place, there are two areas – not unique to us – that bring great frustration to our lives.

The first is our dependency upon supermarket food. We, like most of western society, do not limit ourselves to seasonal or local produce. (40% of the food consumed in the UK is imported from overseas.) We buy potatoes imported from Israel, carrots grown in Egypt, green beans from Kenya, blackberries from Argentina, peas from Zambia, and broccoli from Zimbabwe; not to mention eggs laid by miserable, sore-bottomed chickens that are supposedly fresh but whose watery contents splurge from their shells like puss from an infected wound. It's not appetising and it's not right. Sure, the supermarkets don't help the situation, but we're to blame for creating the demand.

The second area is the volume of food we waste. I was brought up to believe that wasting food is a mortal sin. Yet Mrs H and I throw away bin-loads of uncooked food each week (contributing to the desperate problem that we, as a nation, have only another five years' worth of landfill space left in the UK). We managed to reduce our waste by curbing what we bought, and starting off a little compost heap in the garden so to recycle what was left. But with us both working long hours, it became difficult to plan meals and cook efficiently. And the composting was a disaster. Without any hedges or many shrubs in the garden to provide clippings, we were unable to add enough combustible material to the 'daily peelings'. So they ended up oozing out of the heap and making the garden smell like a sewer.

A change was required. A lifestyle change. To shock us out of the 'convenience store' and 'dustbin man' mentality. We needed guidance. And so, in a quest for faith, we turned to the bible of healthy living.

John Seymour's 'The Complete Book of Self-Sufficiency' and its companion 'Fat of the Land' should be on the bookshelf of anyone seeking a balanced and healthy life. They are the classics that inspired a generation to dig up their gardens and grow vegetables, keep livestock, compost their waste, forage, brew, bake, preserve, build, and learn all the skills needed to live independently of the system. They are reference books, guides, and a roadmap to a better way of living, using the crafts that have mostly been lost by 'advanced' society.

Over a bottle of (shop-bought) wine, Mrs H and I pored over Seymour's books. We learned about the eight pointers to a healthy plot, the principal jobs to do in each season, what can be reasonably expected from plots of different sizes, how to work that land, what to grow (and how to grow it), animal husbandry and butchery, how to hunt and forage, store and preserve food, generate energy and manage waste, and – perhaps most importantly – the essential checklists of why and how someone could become self-sufficient and how they can measure their success. With the exception of John Seymour's slightly New Age references to 'Spaceship Earth', we found his messages to be life changing.

"Self-sufficiency," he says, "is not only for those who have five acres of their own country…However limited the space available, you only need the determination to abandon your space-wasting lawn and flowerbeds in exchange for a programme of planned crop rotation for every inch of your garden to become a productive unit. You will save money, your end products will be fresh, and your garden will be a fine example of a dying breed: the cottage garden of yesteryear."

There were three areas of this statement that most resonated with us. First was that a self-sufficient garden is more about us having determination than surplus space. (Mel Bartholomew's Square Foot Gardening demonstrates this, proving that a 4ft square raised bed with suitable soil – one third compost, one third peat, and one third vermiculite – can be intensely productive, so long as the soil mix is well-watered and replenished each year.) Second was that we could save money and, in the process, become healthier. (Just what we need to beat the supermarket blues.) Thirdly, and most importantly, we would have a garden of yesteryear.

William Lawson, author of A New Orchard and Garden, wrote, "What was paradise, but a garden full of vegetables and herbs and pleasure? Nothing there but delights." The book, which was published in 1618, is one of the earliest classics of gardening literature. Yet Lawson is writing nostalgically of a garden – The Garden of Eden – some four hundred years ago. (His sentiments are especially relevant today, when we are more likely to see a paddling pool or a child's trampoline filling a garden than rows of beautiful and edible plants.) It shows how a proper garden, in the cottage garden sense, contains the inspiration, romance, sentiments, and humble charm that Mrs H and I seek at The Priory. It complements our dream of living a traditional rural life, one centred on the home and the old-fashioned values that enable a peaceful and respectful existence. With all the pieces in place, including 'a garden of yesteryear', we could attain a good life here at Priory HQ.

(Apologies to River Cottage for borrowing the 'HQ' title. But I'm acknowledging the great work they do. While Hugh Fearnley-Whittingstall and crew are best known for championing local, seasonal, and ethically produced food, Fennel's Priory answers the question of 'So, if you did live at River Cottage, what would you do when you'd finished filling your face with food?')

A toast, then, to The Good Life, one enabled by how we perceive and interact with the world around us. May we begin our journey at the heart of our home: our garden (however small or large it may be), because, as John Seymour said, "A true home should be the container for reviving real hospitality, true culture and conviviality, real fun, solid comfort, and above all, real civilisation. And the most creative thing that anybody can do in this world is to make a real home."

So, pick up your packets of seeds (where the past is stored in little envelopes) and sow the dreams of tomorrow.

December

XIV

GARDEN OF DREAMS

> *"In my garden there is a large place for sentiment. My garden of flowers is also my garden of thoughts and dreams. The thoughts grow as freely as the flowers, and the dreams are as beautiful."*
>
> Abram L. Urban

John Seymour's books are the undisputed bibles of self-sufficiency, but the book that began my dream of a simple life was Elizabeth West's Hovel in the Hills. My parents read this to me when I was young, and it inspired me as much as Tolkien's The Hobbit and Lewis' Narnia chronicles. Hovel is not a romanticised view of a self-sufficient life, more a down-to-earth and entirely unsentimental account of an English couple's move to the wilds of North Wales. Here they faced the expected challenges of severe weather and poor soil, and learned that a weed can be prettier – and considerably hardier – than an ornamental plant. But the thing they discovered, and which I took from the book, was the importance of time.

In the opening chapter of her book, Elizabeth West explains the reason behind why she and her husband felt compelled to improve the quality of their lives: "At the time of our marriage we were dutiful slaves of The System. We were both firmly manacled to secure jobs and wrapped up in various hobbies…It took us only a few months to sort out our values. We decided that we did not want a new semi-detached house, a car, a television set, nor expensive furnishings; and our hobbies were only palliatives to a way of life that was becoming more and more pointless. The thing we both wanted, and were noticeably short of, was time. Time to think; time to ponder upon what life was all about."

I was reminded of West's words this morning as, for the sixth morning in succession, I rose early to write the Journal.

('Early' for me is 2.30am – two hours before I would normally rise. And as my departure for work requires me to leave the house at 7.30am, I've had five hours in which to write each morning.)

I have averaged two chapters, four cups of tea, and two rounds of toast per morning, and have so far written fourteen chapters (including a bonus story for the eBook), with a further three left to do. Another morning's work should suffice, but this is time I do not have. Even though today is the 14th December, a Saturday. I am a day late submitting the Journal to the printers, and at great risk of missing the last post before Christmas. I ought to be stressed-out, and thinking of skipping my fifth cup of tea so that I can write an extra hundred words, but I'm not. I am in a slightly dream-like state, partly though lack of sleep and partly because of the stories within this Journal.

GARDEN OF DREAMS

This 'Gardener's Year' is, as I mentioned at the beginning, about dreams. And while Elizabeth West sought time to ponder the purpose of life, I seek time to dream. Which is why, at 10.24am, I have a cup of tea in one hand and a plate of toast in the other. My feet are up, and I am dreaming of my perfect garden.

This garden, which inspires my boldest gardening activities, is not real. It is imagined. Its image has evolved over the years. At one point, in my early teens, it had the most immaculate lawn and weed-free borders; in my twenties it contained clipped yew hedges, roses and a fountain that gushed water thirty feet into the air; in my early thirties it contained a vast lake, surrounded by specimen trees and parkland. And then, a few years ago, the garden – following a year of neglect – became a wildflower meadow filled with buttercups, clover and cow parsley.

During the course of this year, the garden has been carefully managed and cultivated. There's now a sensitive balance between what is ornamental, what is productive, and what is wild. This suits my expectations, and the amount of time I have to tend to its needs. (While you might think that a garden of dreams could morph at the twitch of an eye, the purpose of my imaginary garden is to encourage me to spend as much time as possible tending to it in real time. Each task takes as long as it takes. Trimming the hedges might require me to sit, with my eyes closed, for an entire day. Weeding the borders, or digging the vegetable plot, might take a morning, and sitting in my garden, doing nothing but reflecting upon how beautiful it is, may take no more than an hour. My garden of dreams is where I go, and what I do, when I want to relax. And yet, almost without exception, when I open my eyes and return to the real world I feel compelled to roll up my sleeves and head outdoors in an attempt to bring my real garden somewhere closer to that of my dreams.

GARDEN OF DREAMS

In 1897, Mrs C. W. Earle wrote, "Half the interest of a garden is the constant exercise of the imagination." I like this, as it supports Mary Cantwell's statement that gardeners dream bigger dreams than emperors. But as Dale Carnegie wrote, "One of the most tragic things I know about human nature is that all of us tend to put off living. We are all dreaming of some magical rose garden over the horizon instead of enjoying the roses that are blooming outside our windows today." This is the danger of being a dreamer – that we are always dreaming, and never satisfied with what we've got.

I have spent most of my life dreaming, and not nearly enough time living. However, we need dreams to inspire our actions. It's what keeps us going, what makes us endure hardships. Because when we have a dream, we have a goal, and can put in place a plan to make it real. Our lives then have purpose; we are working towards something. As Vita Sackville West said, "The most noteworthy thing about gardeners is that they are always optimistic, always enterprising and never satisfied." It's a well supported fact. W. E. Johns wrote, "One of the most delightful things about a garden is the anticipation it provides," and Marina Schinz wrote "To create a garden is to search for a better world...hope for the future is at the heart of all gardening." It's what fires us up, and drives us to create our gardens – be they real, dreamed, or metaphors for something else.

I will share with you some words that have encouraged me for many years. They are those of the great Geoff Hamilton, 'the gardener's gardener', who – as presenter of BBC's Gardeners' World for 17 years – encouraged me and millions of others to do and be our best in the garden. "Every individual," he wrote, "with thought, patience and a large portion of help from nature, has it in them to create their own private paradise: truly a thing of beauty and a joy for ever."

So what does my private paradise look like today? Well, as we're in December, my garden has the coolness of mint in an iced tea. While the sun is shining, there's still a layer of frost in the shadowy areas of the garden and I can see my breath condensing in the air before my eyes. But it's by no means winter. The roses still have their leaves, as do the honeysuckles and jasmines that twine freely through the hedgerows. The ground is covered in the yellow and orange leaves of autumn, and yet here and there I can see the new growth of cow parsley and nettles. And the air doesn't smell cold, either, if that makes sense. It is still musky and carries the fruitiness of windfall apples in the orchard (which I leave for my imaginary blackbirds and wasps). The lawn is damp, partly through dew and partly because of recent rain. (Yes, it rains in my imaginary garden, too, especially when the real garden is dry.) It squelches underfoot, reminding me that I ought to lay a path across it before I end up with a muddy streak across the grass. And my greenhouse, which up until today was a small aluminium thing, is now a splendid cedar and glass building complete with finials and cold frames. (Hey, it's nearly Christmas, so if I'm going to treat myself, it might as well be now.) It is in here that my gardening year, next year, will begin. I fancy extending the growing season by raising some early French beans and bringing the herb pots indoors through winter.

(This, I feel, will be my area of learning next year. While the bulk of my experience – and dreaming – has been to do with landscape gardening, I really ought to sink my green fingers into the finely-sieved compost that grows and raises such exotic things as aubergines, cucumbers and chillies.)

But greenhouse gardening is a dream within a dream. I could spend all day in that new, misty and beautifully scented building. But I have a Journal to write (and design, and print, and send to my friends) before I can enjoy the gifts of Christmas. I need to return to the real world, and write with greater speed than ever before. (Three thousand words before lunchtime? No problem!) But before I do, there's something I'd like to share with you. It's what I feel when I'm in my garden. While I always ambassador the 'Stop – Unplug – Escape – Enjoy' message of The Priory, whenever I'm wearing my gardening gloves, I add: 'Feel – Think – Plan – Act – Be'. And when I've done all these, I can 'feel, think, plan, act and be' all over again.

One's gardening apprenticeship never ends; that's why it's so rewarding. It's why I spend so much time caring for my garden of dreams, and when I'm not here, I strive to exist for, and in, the moment. This allows me to be 'present'. So while we are dreaming or doing things that make us who we are, we are never vacant; we are never putting off life. We are always somewhere, being the best we can be.

XV

LEARNING FROM THE MASTER

Everyone needs a hero. Someone who inspires, motivates and protects us. Who imparts their knowledge and shares their time. Who cares for us and pushes us to achieve our dreams. Who has faith in us, and wants us to succeed. Who makes us feel proud, and with whom we share a common bond that defies the boundaries of age or background. A person with whom we share the relationship of master and apprentice.

My hero, who taught me more practical advice about gardening than any textbook or college course, was a man named John Braithwaite. I first met John in 1986 when, as a reckless twelve-year-old, I whizzed past his house on my skateboard. I'd just moved in next door and was yelling with excitement at having so much freedom. John, being a retired 69-year-old, liked the rural tranquillity of the neighbourhood, so came running down his driveway, shaking his fist and shouting at me to "Calm it down!" Later, when he saw me cycling to my gardening jobs with a hoe and rake strapped to the crossbar of my bike, he made his peace with me by presenting me with a bag of apples from his garden. They proved to be the most delicious fruit I'd ever tasted. Visits from John became a regular thing, with him knocking the front door of my family home and handing over a seasonal gift from his garden. If either of my parents answered, then he'd shout up the stairs, asking "Is the lad in?" After a few months, with me making constant remarks about the quality of his produce, John agreed to give me a tour of his garden. I didn't realise how privileged I was.

John's garden, when viewed from the road, was an ornate and immaculate display of snowdrops, daffodils, tulips, gladioli, dahlias and heathers. They grew alongside a pergola, through which twined a wisteria, and beneath which grew standard roses. At twenty yards wide by ten yards deep, it was a floral display from the first snowdrops of spring to the purple and pink heathers of winter. His lawn was neatly trimmed and edged, always green, and with mowing stripes that changed direction with each cut. But, as much as I looked, there was never a weed to be found. The garden was impressive testament to John's keen eye, his knowledge of plants, and meticulous pursuit of perfection.

John walked me through the white metal gates of his driveway. To my surprise, he ignored the front garden completely. Instead, he led me to the double doors of his garage. "There's more to gardening than pretty plants," he said, as he opened the garage doors. "A garden has to work for us, putting food on the table throughout the year."

The garage, which was large enough for two cars, a motorbike and a rotovator, was empty of machinery. Instead, the floor was covered, chest high, with potatoes.

"Oh – my – word!" I exclaimed, while taking a step

back. "How many spuds are there?"

"About four tons," replied John, "give or take a half-hundredweight. Enough to keep me and my sister fed through the winter."

"You never grew all these yourself?" I asked.

"Yes," replied John, "and I'm expecting half as much again in apples, damsons, runner beans and strawberries. In fact, this year alone, I've had over sixty pounds of strawberries from the garden. It's been a good year for fruit and veg, especially when you see what I have to work with."

John then closed the garage doors, smiled confidently, and walked me to the rear of his house. This was the first time I'd seen his back garden. It was approximately four times the size of his front garden, and, with the exception of a small lawn, pond and border next to the house, was dedicated entirely to vegetable and fruit production. A concrete path led down the centre of the garden to a cedar-framed greenhouse. On the right of the path grew runner beans, peas, broad beans, strawberries, rhubarb, gooseberries, blackcurrants and raspberries; on the left grew Brussels sprouts, cabbages, broccoli, turnips, radishes, spring onions, leeks, marrows, lettuce, parsnips, and beetroot. The greenhouse was filled from floor to ceiling with tomatoes, and behind it stood cold frames and compost bins. The far boundary hedge contained apple, pear and damson trees, which were pruned to encourage maximum cropping. The whole scene was overwhelming. Just so much greenery and fruit – all growing for the purpose of feeding its master.

"Er, John," I enquired. "Is there something you're

not telling me?" Of course, John was too modest to answer. It was years before I learned that he was a legend in local horticultural circles. He'd won the village and district's gardening award for ornamental and vegetable growing, flower displays and 'best in class' gardens, every year for nearly thirty years. He was the undisputed champion, the area's top gardener, known affectionately as 'Green Fingers John'. But instead of boasting of his achievements, he began sharing his activities with me in a very hands-on, practical way. He taught me everything from layering strawberries to liming the soil before planting it with brassicas. And, a source of constant humour, he was infinitely stronger than me, even though he was nearly a foot shorter, and sixty years older, than me. So, as I 'fiddled about', as he put it, digging with a spade, he would manhandle the grunting, churning, vibrating beast of a rotovator through the soil. (It was the largest I'd ever seen. A 1948 BMB Plowmate. At 900 ccs and 10 horsepower, it could have doubled as a small tractor.) John's energy – and knowledge – was limitless, a benefit of real life experience rather than desk-based learning.

When I applied to go to horticultural college, at the age of 19, John invited me round to his house for 'a cup of tea and a chat'. He was clearly excited that his protégé was seeking to become a 'proper' gardener.

"Fennel," said John, "this garden was built by me in 1930, with my own hands. I have used these hands to work the soil every day since then. If there's one thing I've learned, that's more important than anything else, and which I want you to understand, is that you need to work the soil to make it work for you. I was a farm labourer and manager for my entire working life, and had access to an endless supply of pig manure. I could tell, just from the smell, which slurry pit had been opened, and when it was ready to go on the garden. You shouldn't be able to see my house for the muck I've put on this garden over the years. There's sixty years' worth on those borders and veg plots. That's why my plants do so well. So keep this knowledge in your mind when those lecturers fill your head with stuff they've read in books.

I remember returning from college one summer, and telling John about the things I'd learned. I excitedly explained the process of 'warm bath' treatment for eradicating nematodes from daffodil bulbs; about how light passing through leaves of plants is filtered, coming out the other side as invisible 'far red' light that inhibits plant growth beneath the canopy; how micro propagation of plant cell tissue can grow hundreds of plants from a single parent leaf; and that early-mid spring is the best time to take cuttings, due to the concentration of growth hormones in the growing tips.

John leaned forward and said, "My boy, the best time to take cuttings…is when nobody's looking. Get into the habit of going for a dawn walk; take a rifle and bag a pheasant or two, then return home with the birds over your shoulder and the gun on your arm. That way, no bugger will challenge you if they see you rummaging through their daffodil borders looking for prize-winning specimens." He paused, and then said, "You never ought to pay for an ornamental plant, not if you've got green fingers. You grow them yourself, as a matter of pride. Though of course, vegetables are different: you have to select or buy-in the best seed to get the best crops."

Put properly in my place, I decided never again to brag about anything I learned in class. Instead I only ever spoke to John about things I'd experienced firsthand, or wished to learn from him.

Sadly, in the late 1990s, I went in search of bright lights and fool's gold. I left home, and distanced myself from my friends. I barely saw John during this time. And then, in December 1999, I visited him with a Christmas card and present. He was unshaven, hobbling on weakened legs, and had a chesty cough which he found annoying. We spoke about his garden, and the extra heating he'd needed for the greenhouse due to the cold winter. He pointed at the three-bar electric fire, saying how it was his only heating in the house other than the coal fire in the living room. He'd resorted to wearing an extra pair of socks and his bobble hat indoors. But he didn't grumble. It was all part of country life to him. He'd lived in that house, with his elder sister, for nearly seventy years. We joked, told stories, and then shook hands, just as we'd done many times before. I left for home; feeling like our friendship was stronger than ever. But it was short-lived. Soon after, I had a telephone call from my mother saying that John was in hospital. His cough had developed into a serious condition. Before I had chance to visit him, I received another phone call saying he'd died from respiratory failure.

Losing a close friend is tough. But losing one's hero? It leaves an emptiness inside that can never be filled.

While we may go on living, and continuing along the path we walked with them, we cannot help but feel alone, no matter how many friends we have around us. Our guiding light is gone, and we are left fumbling through the darkness.

Darkness rarely lasts forever, at least when we open our eyes and look to the horizon. The light appeared for me this morning when, as I stood looking eastwards at dawn, I thought of John and the words in this Journal. He is the one who should take credit for everything I've written this year: all the fun stuff, all the sincerity, all the horticultural gems and everything that's come from my enthusiasm for gardening. I therefore dedicate this Journal to John Braithwaite, the gardener whom I most respected. His legacy is that gardening – like life – should be simple. Don't overcomplicate it with science, and theory, and reasons why; see it as art, and beauty, and a way of connecting with something very real. So if you do but one thing after reading this Journal, purchase a packet of seeds and grow some food for your table. Remember: John is watching over you, so make sure you've got a garage big enough for your harvest.

THE LAST CAST

As an angler I'm entitled to one last cast, a final attempt to capture what I seek to convey. So here goes:

Frederick Eden wrote, "A garden is not made in a year; indeed it is never made in the sense of finality. It grows, and with the labour of love should go on growing." This is its gift to us. A perpetual promise of futures green. Of happy days with trowel, fork, and barrow. The Journal, therefore, is about the future and all the joy it can bring. That said, I'm grateful of the years of pleasure that gardening has already brought to me. Thirty-five years and counting. From my earliest days in my play garden, to the elegant stately homes of England and now to my own humble plot, my love has remained constant. I have always enjoyed and looked forward to every task. From shovelling manure in winter to mowing lawns in summer; planning the subtle (and sometimes dramatic) changes in the garden, and noting how they made me feel; I was a gardener throughout. Mine is a gardener's life which, if I'm lucky and healthy, is only half done. There's plenty left to do.

"Gardening is a long road," wrote Henry Mitchell, "with many detours and way stations, and here we all are at one point or another. It's not a question of superior or inferior taste, merely a question of which detour we are on at the moment. Getting there (as they say) is not important; the wandering about in the wilderness or in the olive groves or in the bayous is the whole point." This gives me pleasure, and reminds me that gardening is the great leveller. It doesn't matter who we are, or where we garden; we are bound by our love of plants and outdoor spaces. We are Nature's helpers, custodians of things that provide life-giving oxygen and great pleasure to those who see, hear, feel and breathe. That's pretty much everyone. So while we may convince ourselves that we garden for only our benefit, everything we do has broader value. Our gardens reflect us, and us them, repaying our efforts with smiling flowers, wholesome crops and clean air. We give, they give. It's a simple as that. And if we don't get things right first time, then it doesn't matter. Gardening is one of the few hobbies where it's perfectly okay to be absolutely rubbish at what we do. There's always a second chance to put right our mistakes, and perfect what we've done. Time and Nature are most forgiving.

Nancy Ross wrote, "My spirit was lifted and my soul nourished by my time in the garden. It gave me a calm connection with all of life, and an awareness that remains with me now, long after leaving the garden." I hope this is how you feel, now the Journal is ending. But spring will soon be here, and with it a new growing season – full of flowers, adventures and dreams.

ABOUT THE AUTHOR

FENNEL HUDSON

"Author, artist, naturalist and countryman. His is a lifestyle to inspire the most bricked-up townie."

Fennel Hudson is a lifestyle and countryside author known for his *Fennel's Journal* books and *Contented Countryman* podcasts. A green-fingered naturalist, his gardens exist in wild and domestic places – some of them in metaphor and all seeking to enrich the beauty of our world. He began his gardening career at the age of 11, with a Saturday job that 'paid little but rewarded greatly'. He then worked on large country estates before training in horticulture – something that would enrich his appreciation of the natural world. After college he worked as a garden designer, then for landscape firms, garden centres and plant nurseries. He changed career in his mid-thirties, becoming a writer who seeks to create 'a garden of words'. Always pausing to smell the roses, his motto is 'Stop – Unplug – Escape – Enjoy'.

For more information please visit:
www.fennelspriory.com

THE FENNEL'S JOURNAL SERIES

Fennel's Journal

Issue 1 · Christmas 2006

The Meaning of Life

THE FIRST-EVER REVIEWS OF FENNEL'S JOURNAL:

"Fennel's Journal began as a series of illustrated letters to friends. As these evolved they became less a diary, more a manifesto, and the Journal is now exactly that – a way of living, rurally and simply: very real for all those who recognise the importance of tradition and joy."

Caught by the River

"I can see where it might lead. What he has would make amazing TV. It's the Good Life, but in a realistic way. It's Jack Hargreaves. It's Countryfile. It's quality Sunday newspaper stuff. It's 1948, all over again. In trying to escape the present he's inevitably created a brand. A potentially very powerful brand."

Bob Roberts Online

"Fennel's Journal is a masterpiece about rural living. It is a route-map to the life we all seek."

The Traditional Fisherman's Forum

From A Meaningful Life:

"Life is the most beautiful and rewarding gift. We just need to take time out to allow us to reflect, change perspective, and see things in their best light. Sometimes we just have to stop and feel the pulse of the Earth, the rhythm of the seasons and the internal voice that was once our childhood friend. As the natural world grows smaller, so too does its intensity and the size of the window through which it may be viewed."

NO.1

A MEANINGFUL LIFE

A Meaningful Life is the first and perhaps most important Journal. It documents the origins of Fennel's Priory and why Fennel decided to live by a new set of ideals. With themes ranging from escapism, adventure, work-life balance, identity and purpose, through to traditionalism and country living, it sets the scene for future editions – building messages that are central to Fennel's Priory. Ultimately it conveys the importance of a relaxed, balanced, and meaningful life.

READER TESTIMONIALS

"I loved reading this Journal. It's inspiring and has the beginnings of something very special."

"Fennel's chosen trajectory is firmly in the slow lane. He's a countryman, with courage to stand behind his traditional values."

"Witty and emotive, Fennel's writing conveys passion for a slower-paced and quieter life."

From A Waterside Year:

"Water is intrinsically linked to the mystery and excitement of discovering new worlds. Of dreams. And hopes. And thoughts of what 'could be'. Dreams free us from normality. ...As the daydreams grew longer, the distinction between what was real and what was imaginary grew less. Soon I existed in a blissful world of my own creation. Reality, as I learned, is only a matter of perception...A life that is real to one is surreal to another."

NO. 2

A WATERSIDE YEAR

In *A Waterside Year*, Fennel takes time out to live beside a lake in rural England. Here he appreciates the healing qualities of water, studies the wildlife around him, lives at the pace of someone outside of normal daily life, and discovers the freedom that's found in isolation. Getting so close to Nature, and spending time in idle fashion, enables him to discover a stronger sense of self. Ultimately he learns that freedom is not a place, but something that exists within us.

READER TESTIMONIALS

"A year in the wild. How we would all love to follow in Fennel's stead and indulge our dreams, to come out the other side a stronger and wiser person."

"A Journal with a message – that we should take time out to think about what's important, and see the beauty of the world."

"A truly blissful read full of inspiration and humour. The story of Fennel sitting in his tent, with the noises outside, had me laughing out loud!"

From A Writer's Year:

"Writing, with a fountain pen and ink from a bottle, is the simplest of things. Yet it can transport us to a different place entirely. Imagination is the real magic that exists in this world. Look inwards, to see outwards. And capture it in writing."

NO. 3

A WRITER'S YEAR

A Writer's Year celebrates the writer's craft. It champions the handwritten letter, discusses vintage pens and writing ink, and celebrates things such as antique typewriters and the quirkiness of the creative mind. It's a blend of observations. It's funny. It's serious. It's real life. But most of all it is written to encourage aspiring authors to find their voice, to put pen to paper, and follow their dreams.

READER TESTIMONIALS

"Worth it for the first chapter alone. It cannot fail to motivate and inspire the would-be author."

"What Fennel has written is not so much a eulogy for the handwritten letter as a call-to-arms for everyone to follow their dreams and make the most of their God-given talents. This is a genuinely inspiring read."

"I loved the part: 'If a pen can communicate our thoughts, dreams and emotions and be the voice of our soul, then ink is the medium that carries the message'. It shows how important and generous writing can be."

From Wild Carp:

"Some will say that searching for your dreams is like looking for unicorns in an emerald forest. They will say that following a golden thread will lead only to a king, dethroned and living in the gutter. This may be so.
But the king was made, not born.
The crown was never his to wear.
...If ever the adventure proves tiring, or you lose sight of your dream, look to the west at sunset. There, on days when the skies are clear, you might see upon the horizon a thin layer of golden mist. When it appears, you will know its purpose: it is
the mist of believing."

NO. 4

WILD CARP

Angling for wild carp is about adventure, history, atmosphere and emotion. *Wild Carp* captures this aplenty, describing Fennel's 20-year quest to find a very special type of fish. But it's also about nature connection and a desire to uncover the seemingly impossible – a place where we can discover and live out our dreams, to completely indulge the mantra of 'Stop – Unplug – Escape – Enjoy'.

READER TESTIMONIALS

"When written well, traditional angling writing by the likes of BB, for example, is the type of literature that I can read again and again. Fennel's writing flows un-hurried without overly romanticising each point and the research is thorough; from the first sentence I was thinking, 'this lad can write!' It's informative and very refreshing."

"Such inspiring writing. His words 'Somewhere in the undergrowth of the impossible' had me staring out from the page in amazement. Fennel's writing is pure poetry."

From Fly Fishing:

"The deeper we travel into the natural world, and the greater the number of technological encumbrances we leave behind, the more likely we are to escape the fast-paced lifestyle and stresses of the 21st Century.
For some, angling enables a quest into the unknown, an adventure into the wild. For these fortunate folk, fly-fishing is escapism. Their hours by water serve as contemplation to enrich their souls, directing their quest inwards, towards their longed-for state of completeness."

NO. 5

FLY FISHING

Fly Fishing celebrates the most graceful and artful form of angling, explaining what it means to be an angler – in the spirit of Izaak Walton – and how fly fishers differ from bait fishers. The sporting and aesthetic beauty of fly-fishing is described in Fennel's usual witty and contemplative style. As he says, "Fly fishing is the ultimate form of angling; it gives us a reason to fish simply, travel lightly, and explore wild places that replenish our soul. With a fly rod, we're not casting to a fish; rather to a circle of dreams: ripples that spread into every aspect of our lives".

READER TESTIMONIALS

"Brilliant writing. Fennel made me laugh out loud in bed. My wife was asking questions!"

"A delightful, well-articulated, read. I strongly recommend it, especially to the contemplative, tradition-loving, bamboo fly rod devotees among us."

"A very inspiring and rewarding read. I will try to tie the Sedgetastic fly. It looks tasty!"

From Traditional Angling:

"Physics teaches us that for every action, there is an equal and opposite reaction: a natural balance of energy that sustains the equilibrium of life. In modern angling, these forces are skewed so far in favour of technology that the balance between science and art has been lost. But there is a movement, an undercurrent that defies the flow of progress. There are those who choose not to follow the crowd. They seek not to fish in a predictable, scientific manner. They yearn for the opposite, to buck the trend, *to be different*. They are the Traditional Anglers."

NO. 6

TRADITIONAL ANGLING

Traditional Angling celebrates the Waltonian values of angling: about fishing in a seasonal and uncompetitive way for the pure pleasure of being beside water. It wears its heart on its sleeve and a wildflower in its lapel. It's passionate, provocative and eccentric, written for those who appreciate the aesthetics of angling and uphold its sporting traditions. So, with great enthusiasm, raise your bamboo rod aloft for an adventure that proves there's more to fishing than catching fish.

READER TESTIMONIALS

"A beautifully written, very engaging and hugely enjoyable read. In fact, it's the best thing on fishing I've read in a long time."

"What a Journal! Fennel is clearly the spiritual successor to his mentor – the great Bernard Venables. There's so much wisdom and craftsmanship in his writing. Bernard clearly taught him very well."

From The Quiet Fields:

"The countryside, with its vast horizons, fresh air and ever-changing seasons is, by its very nature, more life-giving and adventurous than any amount of modern indoor living. It inspires a love of natural history – everything from the birds that sing in the trees to the quality and richness of the soil beneath our feet. Most of all, it creates the desire to exist more naturally. And in doing so, we appreciate the balance of life."

NO. 7

THE QUIET FIELDS

The Quiet Fields is rooted in the humus-rich soil of the countryside. It's about remote rural places where Nature exists undisturbed, where we may sit and ponder 'The Wonder of the World'. The Journal tips its hat to these places, and to the nature writing of BB, revealing the 'Lost England' that still exists if you know where and how to look. It is the most sentimental and astutely observed Journal to date, discussing the 'true beauty' of Nature. If you've ever yearned to hear birdsong during a busy day, then this is the book for you.

READER TESTIMONIALS

"Fennel's writing reminds me of the works of Roger Deakin. It inspires me with faith in the quiet life and that although I may be isolated, I am certainly not alone."

"Fennel has captured the essence of the countryside – that is, its almost human character. So brilliantly has he compared and contrasted it with the nature of we humans. It's not so much a 'balanced study', more a 'study of the balance' between Nature and Man."

From Fine Things:

"It seems that, depending upon which side of the thesaurus-writer's gaze we sit, one's uniqueness as a person can be deemed to be either eccentric or distinctive. Both, in my opinion, are good...As we get older, and experience more things, those of us with strength of character and a sense of purpose will grow stronger and fight harder; those who lack identity and direction might end up sitting in a corner somewhere, blindly taking all the knocks that life throws at them. What does this teach us? That character and purpose are directly linked to confidence and conviction. What links them? Courage – to be oneself, no matter what others might say."

NO. 8

FINE THINGS

Fine Things celebrates the special and sentimental items and activities that convey our personality. The writing is fast-paced, quirky and humorous, reflecting the author's enthusiasm and eccentric view of the world. But be warned: if you look inside Fennel's mind, you might see a hula-hooping hamster named Gerald, shaking his maracas, loudly banging a bongo, and getting him into all sorts of trouble. So strap yourself in. This book picks up pace and takes some unexpected turns. From the deeply personal to the outright eccentric, it's for those who seek to be different.

READER TESTIMONIALS

"A very fine thing, indeed. Fennel's best and funniest book to date. He is the only author who can make me laugh out loud and cry in the same sentence. I was constantly in tears, for all the right reasons."

"Deep in places, outright bonkers in others. A demonstration of the fine line between genius and madness."

From A Gardener's Year:

"Roll up your sleeves and imagine your vision of paradise. This, in whatever form it takes, is your garden. Keep hold of the image; know it's every detail and piece together the elements that need creating or nurturing, so that when you get the chance, you can prepare the ground, sow the seeds, and make it real. Ours is a gardener's life, whether we realise it or not."

NO. 9

A GARDENER'S YEAR

A Gardener's Year celebrates the joy of growing things and reflects upon a life working with plants. But it's not a record of horticultural activities through the seasons. It's a metaphor for having a dream and making it come true. For Fennel, who has spent half his life working in gardens, it's about cultivating a cottage garden where he can aspire to a self-sufficient lifestyle. The Journal sees him sow the seeds of this future reality.

READER TESTIMONIALS

"Fennel's writing is uniquely funny. I mean, who else can name a chapter 'Chicken Poo'? His sense of humour, balanced with some deep yet subtle messages, had me in tears. From his 'escape' to a public toilet, to what not to say to a celebrity, this is a Journal to entertain all readers."

"When I started reading this Journal I had a garden with a lawn and a patio. Now I have a vegetable patch, blisters, an aching back, and the biggest smile of my life. Thank you Fennel!"

From The Lighter Side:

"If self-actualisation is the pinnacle of one's development, then it can't be achieved if your mountain has two peaks...Being the 'best version' of yourself implies that you have other versions kept locked in a closet. Don't have any 'versions'. Just have one true, beautiful and pure form of you.
So climb your mountain, open your arms to the Creator who greets you there, and sing loudly to the world that stretches out beneath you. Write your name permanently on the landscape of your mind. Remember: you are a child of Nature. And you are free."

NO. 10

THE LIGHTER SIDE

There's a delicate balance between something meaning a great deal and that same thing becoming so serious that it's ludicrous. (Ever got stressed about what clothes to wear for an interview?) That's why *The Lighter Side* provides the encouragement, humour, anecdotes, reflections and honesty that are essential to Fennel's message of 'Stop – Unplug – Escape – Enjoy'. After all, we can only 'Enjoy' if we know how to smile when we get there.

READER TESTIMONIALS

"The Lighter Side was more than I expected. The deeper meaning within it – and the devastating honesty it conveys – made me question exactly where I am in my own life and what I can do to improve it for my family and me in the time that remains. Thank you Fennel for opening my eyes and adjusting my course."

"The opening chapter is the most startling, erudite, compassionate and open piece of writing I have ever read…thank you Fennel for sharing so much. It did and does mean a great deal."

From Friendship:

"What I'm talking about is proper friendship. The sort that is authentic, genuine and real. Where we can look into the eyes of another person and know what they're thinking. ...Because, as friends, we remember 'why' as much as 'when' or 'what'. Through good times and bad, we were there. Together. That's the bond, the unquestionable obligation that's freely given. It's the tightest hug, the biggest kiss, the tearful hello and the widest smile. If that's what it means to be a friend, or an extrovert, or just someone who cares for others then that's me to the last beat of my heart."

NO. 11

FRIENDSHIP

Written by the Friends of the Priory, with bonus chapters from Fennel, *Friendship* provides insights into what it means to be friends, how shared interests and beliefs support collective purpose, and how, when we're together, we can achieve more, appreciate more, and have more fun. It's about the broader world of Fennel's Priory and how it exists in others. It's a book written 'for us by us', with friendship as the theme.

READER TESTIMONIALS

"Possibly the greatest gift that this Journal bestows is to let us know that we are not alone."

"Like friendship itself, this Journal brings together people and meaning. It reminds us that 'together we are strong'. Thank you Fennel for leading our charge."

"The message (and evolution) of Fennel's Journal is most evident in this Friendship edition. With such obvious themes as identity and legacy, it's clear that what Fennel has shared over the years is a route-map to freedom and a stronger sense of self."

From Nature Escape:

"I am once again seeking an escape, to where I hope to find freedom and connect with the young man who handed me his trust ten years ago. This will be a faithful interpretation of the Priory, a fitting way to mark ten years of writing. As I said at the end of last year's Journal, 'One's journey through life is not linear; it's circular.' So let's go back to the beginning, and rediscover the quiet world."

NO. 12

NATURE ESCAPE

Nature Escape provides the most detailed account of a day that follows the motto of 'Stop – Unplug – Escape – Enjoy'. In it Fennel returns to the woodland of his youth to study its wildlife and savour its peacefulness.

Written in real-time, with twenty-four chapters that each represent an hour, the Journal is an account of how time spent outdoors in wild places enables us to observe the nature that's around us *and* within us.

READER TESTIMONIALS

"Fennel's Journal has always provided us with an escape, but now we know where the escape can lead. As promised, it leads to enjoyment – and very enjoyable it is too!"

"24 hours alone in a wood, with only 'the wild' for company? With Fennel as our guide, there's no such thing as 'alone'; only the warmth of knowing that quiet times are the fine times."

"By studying the nature within us and around us, Fennel demonstrates how to be 'at one' with nature."

From Book of Secrets:

"There's a greater man than me who can sum up our journey, a mountaineer who in 1865 first climbed the Matterhorn. Edward Whymper, over to you: 'There have been joys too great to be described in words, and there have been griefs upon which I have not dared to dwell, and with these in mind I say, climb if you will, but remember that courage and strength are naught without prudence, and that a momentary negligence may destroy the happiness of a lifetime. Do nothing in haste, look well to each step, and from the beginning think what may be the end.'"

NO. 13

BOOK OF SECRETS

Book of Secrets links all editions of Fennel's Journal together. With 14 Journals in the series, and 14 core chapters in this book, it's the 'one book to bind them all' with each chapter providing the continuity story from one Journal to the next.

Containing Fennel's previously private writing, it provides deep insight into the Fennel's Journal story. If you've ever wondered why each Journal is themed the way it is, or tried to find the metaphor in each edition, then *Book of Secrets* is for you.

READER TESTIMONIALS

"What a privilege: being able to read the private writing of my favourite author. Book of Secrets is a treat."

"Such honesty and wit. Fennel puts into words what I have only ever thought, or dare not say."

"Fennel's Journal really is a series – it's meant to be read as a whole. And now we have the key to unlock it."

From The Pursuit of Life:

"We can hide, or we can strive – for a life of our making. With endless possibilities and opportunities to reach for our dreams, we owe it to ourselves to dream big and keep going, irrespective of what we might encounter. Sadly, the thing that most limits our success is not others, but ourselves. How strongly we believe, how confidently we act, how fiercely we react, how passionately we want, and how life-affirmingly compelled we are to grow and blossom; that's how we keep going, no matter what, to be the person we want to be, living the life we deserve, in dreams that are real."